DIVING FOR
PEARLS

EXPLORING PHILOSOPHY WITH MY FATHER

Diving for Pearls: Exploring Philosophy with my Father

Copyright 2021 by Thomas Brockelman

First printing 2021

$16.95

Standing Stone Books is an imprint of **Standing Stone Studios,**
an organization dedicated to the promotion of the literary and visual arts.

Mailing address:
1897 State Route 91, Fabius, New York 13063

Web address:
standingstonebooks.net

Email:
standingstonebooks@gmail.com

Distributor:
Small Press Distribution
1341 Seventh Avenue
Berkeley, California 94710-1409
Spdbooks.org

ISBN: 9781637609132

Library of Congress Control Number: 2020951685

Book Design by Adam Rozum

Standing Stone Books is a member of the Community of Literary Magazines and Presses
Clmp.org

Thomas Brockelman

DIVING FOR
PEARLS

EXPLORING PHILOSOPHY WITH MY FATHER

Standing Stone Books

For Mira,
who loved and challenged Paul Brockelman equally.

Acknowledgments

Many people and institutions were helpful in bringing *Diving for Pearls* to completion. A retreat for writing and spirituality sponsored by Le Moyne College set me solidly on the road to this book, convincing me that I had a story to tell in the midst of mourning for my father. In particular, let me thank William Redfield, who facilitated the retreat, and Maura Brady and Dan Roche of Le Moyne College for organizing the event. Dan also read an early draft of my manuscript, and his encouragement and positive feedback was pivotal. My thanks also to numerous friends and colleagues at Le Moyne College, whose encouragement has varied in form from hallway discussions to funding a generous sabbatical largely dedicated to working through my manuscript.

Speaking of that revision, novelist and memoirist Andrew J. Krivak read through an entire draft, offering criticisms inspirational for a radical re-working of the project; his later praise for the revised manuscript also sparked the idea that I might actually publish writing of a kind distant from my normal academic comfort zone. Syracuse's YMCA Downtown Writer's Center has one of the most vibrant programs in the country for helping budding writers along: a non-fiction class there with Nancy Keefe Rhodes allowed me to workshop a number of *Diving*'s meditations, the feedback from which was vital for the book's final shape. Keefe Rhodes also returned with an enormously helpful final edit of the nearly finished manuscript. She pruned my often flowery prose into something more resembling the English language we all speak together.

Philosopher friends and colleagues Richard Boothby and Anthony Steinbock both supported the project and encouraged its publication. My immediate family, Rachel and Sophie, have kept me going on this road when I was tempted to give it up, and my sister, Mira, was gracious both in challenging my memory and cheering the project on.

Finally, I'd like to thank Robert Colley of Standing Stone Books, who was willing to take on publication of a book that seems to fall between the cracks of normal publication categories. Bob has been tireless and professional in bringing my manuscript to its full potential.

Portrait of Paul Brockelman
by Adeline Goldminc-Tronzo

Paul Brockelman (1935-2016) was a distinguished Professor of Philosophy at the University of New Hampshire from 1963-2001. He was an active scholar, authoring, translating or co-editing seven books, including *Existential Phenomenology and the World of Experience: An Introduction; Time and Self: Phenomenological Explorations;* and *The Greening of Faith: God, the Environment, and the Good Life.* He was also an exceptionally successful and well-loved teacher, winning several prestigious teaching awards throughout his career. Paul graduated from Philips Andover Academy and Dartmouth College, graduating with a B.A. in Eastern Religions, and went on to complete a Ph.D. in philosophy from Northwestern University, where he specialized in Existential Philosophy. His wife of 55 years, Barbara Davis, passed away in 2011, and he is survived by his two children, Thomas and Mira. Thomas, following in his father's footsteps, also became a philosophy professor.

Introduction

I found the manuscript a week after my father died. Even in the midst of his apartment's modest detritus, the neatness and preparation of the box containing his materials struck me, a contrast to the increasingly messy files containing pretty much everything else from his life's last years—bills, correspondence, will. He had also carefully left it *on top* of the filing cabinet containing all those other papers, in a spot where it couldn't be missed, either by his almost-blind single eye or by my own eyes as I cleaned out his belongings.

SEEING LIFE WHOLE AGAIN, said the cover page in the bold 20-point block letters used by the semi-blind. Most of the remainder of that page was taken up with a color reproduction of Gauguin's late painting, "Where do we come from? What are we? Where are we going?" framed below by that painting's title in block letters of equal size and weight to the book's title. Typos riddled the page—a sad testament to the process of writing while blind. Finally, my father had affixed his own name, Paul Brockelman, at the bottom of the page.

There followed some four hundred and twenty pages of text and several spiral bound copies of the manuscript; then there was a hard drive with this and several earlier versions of the book, all from the last years of his life. Dad had clearly been working on this book for a long time. I spent a few moments with the contents of the manuscript box and then set it carefully aside. In a life given over to philosophy, a philosophical manuscript (and one so carefully presented!) must stand out from bills, underwear, and even copies of a will.

The manuscript wasn't a complete surprise. In those last years, even before my mother died, my father had told me about it, mentioning it often in the very last years, as his faculties failed, lights blinking out, one by one. Because I didn't want to disappoint him with my professional judgment of his text, I discouraged any conversation that might lead to his requesting that I read it, even when he hinted, not so subtly, that he would welcome

Title Page for Manuscript
of "Seeing Life Whole Again,"

exactly that. My steering the conversation away from his book was part of a long truce between us, one that demanded—oddly between philosopher father and philosopher son—that the topic of philosophy itself remain on the sidelines.

In the course of his decline, the combativeness in his philosophical personality had gained the upper hand, while his profound deafness forbade any really productive discussion. In that situation, any opportunity to walk on philosophical ground simply became an invitation for him to lecture—usually in the same patronizing way that, earlier in life, he reserved for reprimands about my misbehavior ("Don't you think you need to acknowledge that all philosophy comes from experience? Well, Tom?")

Part of what I already knew about *Seeing Life Whole* was how difficult it was for my father to write. In younger days this spitting image of Abe Lincoln had enjoyed something of Lincoln's calm but dynamic energy. The older Paul Brockelman, wasted to half his earlier weight, and only standing straight with great difficulty, couldn't really muster the concentration to write a book. Moreover, my father had confessed to me repeatedly that his almost-blind, sedated state in those last years condemned him to falling ever further behind scholarship in the many fields his work intersected. He had been a voracious reader in younger days. Now, with the best will, he could only creep through a few pages of somebody's book or article in a day. More than that, he admitted to me that everything he wrote in those last few years had the quality of starting well but, at some point, grinding to a kind of breathless halt.

Unlike his earlier writing projects, he knew "this one" was his last

14

and he knew, somehow, that to "finish" the manuscript would consign him to death, or at least to intellectual morbidity, since nothing following it could count intellectually. Of course, I can't really know what it's like to be where he was—clearly aware of imminent death and needing a "last word." What does it feel like to send such a final message, to gather one's entire life for one's exit?

More than a year after he died, I finally sat down with the book. I could immediately see the effects of Paul's uncertainty. For one thing, the hard drive contained not one but four books, all consisting of similar materials and meditations arranged differently and dated from five years before his death to the last year. All versions were incomplete, with many chapters and sections consisting solely of pasted quotes from books or newspaper articles that he liked, and some of the chapters seemed little more than notes for later writing.

In my efforts to grapple with his manuscript and figure out what my father meant *to me*, I gradually came to see his life as a particular kind of philosophical *drama*: a story of a certain human frailty or weakness transformed into the great human strength of reflection.

In his artful mastery of this transformation, my father's story belongs to the genre of tales of the trickster—the figure who conquers just when and where he seems most profoundly to have lost the game. A sickly child who would go on to suffer from the childhood diseases common in his day as well as at least one near-fatal accident, he nonetheless roared out of Worcester, Massachusetts, embracing all the near-extinction events of his early life and turning them into fuel for the philosopher's view of life. In the repeatedly renewed labor of this transformation I came to see my father's great courage and faith. Ever and again, he would rake up the coals of his suffering, blow gently upon them, and let them burst forth again in courageous flame.

One comment about the *form* of the following, a form made necessary by the peculiar way that my father always erased the boundaries between the personal and the philosophical. Each of the "chapters" in the book is really a "meditation," a form that has existed since the ancient world and one that aims to ground otherwise abstract thought in concrete experience. I am telling the stories of both my father's life and of his thought. This form suggested itself naturally to me as I began to write, promising to make room for both the personal and the philosophical at once.

So each meditation hides both a story about Paul and one of his life insights, burnished as the answer to a basic philosophical question. I am offering to the reader both an orderly set of basic philosophical reflections and an account of Paul Brockelman's life.

In combining the projects of memoir and philosophical meditation, my book is something of a hybrid in its genre. But this odd combination seemed absolutely necessary from the first: a key to Dad's work was his belief in and commitment to philosophizing *from* experience—which meant that his own work at its best was thoroughly full of stories about his own life. Doing justice to Paul Brockelman meant doing philosophy through story, through the story of his life, including his life with me. My own reflections on my father just add another strand to this web of stories.

Oh, and the title: Paul made that up himself, in a light moment, when referring to the permanent alienation that his commitment to experiential philosophizing produced from the scholarly mainstream. I remember asking him, perhaps in my teens, what he was writing at the time. He responded, "This one, I'm definitely holding on to the movie rights!" and continued, "It's definitely, *Diving for Pearls off the Coast of Academia*." "Diving for Pearls" became a kind of family by-word, used for the next project, the one that would finally be a hit, that non-scholars would come to know.

Anyhow, with its appropriate claim to transcend academic form— not to mention its humor—my father's own mythic title seemed well suited to settle on the book just "beyond" the one that he actually wrote, just after his own works.

My own use of philosophical memoir participates in a growing genre. Sarah Bakewell's *At the Existentialist Café* tipped me off to the possibility of writing in this way: I'm sure that it's no coincidence that she felt compelled to combine the concrete history of Existentialism, some of the same philosophy that inspired my father, with story.

Another work that influenced me was John Kaag's *American Philosophy: A Love Story*. Here, too, the author sought to find a way of writing about a philosophy that was key for my father, who loved William James' *Varieties of Religious Experience*. Like existentialism, the traditions of American philosophy that centered John Kaag's study demanded a personal, experiential voice. In Kaag's case, this was the story of what he called his own "erotic" development through the discovery of philosophy. I found Kaag's accounts of his own philosophical loves moving, complete with the story of his courtship with his wife and with numerous discoveries from mouldering Vermont bookshelves.

My point in underscoring both of these works is to applaud a potential direction for philosophy today—a return to the idea that the history of philosophy, more than a series of narrow, specialized doctrines or contributions to knowledge, amounts to a search for *a way of life*, for an elusive (and disputed) synthesis of knowledge and wisdom. I am not questioning the abstraction of philosophy. But mourning my father has powerfully driven home to me the importance of another kind of philosophical work: this search for a life that would stay true to the basic questions of being human.

I don't know what I expected to find or do when I began reading through *Seeing Life Whole Again* on that rainy Sunday morning in April, 2017. I do know that I was in a different place than I was the previous winter when I stumbled upon it. I was somehow ready to pass beyond the rigid truce that my father and I had reached toward the end of his life. I was ready to mourn my father in a way that I hadn't been able to do immediately after of his death and to celebrate his life more fully than before.

It gradually came to me that, as a gift to him, I could help him finish the last book he couldn't complete himself, the one that would be a fitting testimony to his rich life as a thinker and teacher. As it turns out, what you have before you doesn't immediately resemble *Seeing Life Whole Again*, but I hope it tells the story my father wanted to tell.

I also realized that he had *left me* a gift, a chance to return to my relationship with him through his manuscript, to dissolve or shift the boundaries that we had erected between us—boundaries increasingly hemming us both in as I approached middle age and he the end of his life. I could write a kind of philosophical love letter for my father, acknowledging how much he meant to me, both as a son and philosopher. The book in front of you is two things. It is an effort, in celebrating a good life in philosophy, to let my father speak, to bring forth the wonderful voice that hundreds of his students and colleagues remember, and it is my attempt to "work through" (as psychotherapists say) what it meant to be his son.

MEDITATION 1 PHILOSOPHY AND WONDER

How does wonder lead to philosophy?

Forget success in philosophy—as he passed through childhood and youth, it was by no means clear that Paul Brockelman would have a life at all. His mother suffered from "nerves," institutionalized at least twice. His father had the emotional vocabulary of a block of wood and died miserably of pancreatic cancer in his fifties. His brother never entered a serious romantic relationship, never really enjoyed himself, and spent his life burning through the considerable business that he inherited from his father.

Moreover, my father was himself a delicate plant. He survived several childhood diseases (including the measles, probably contributing to his later deafness) that left him weak, sickly. He always told my sister and me of the pain he suffered when he had to watch other nine-year-old boys playing baseball while he remained confined to a wheelchair, a blanket draped, lovingly, over him by his mother. He writes of this moment in *Seeing Life Whole Again*: unable to play with the other boys, he began to notice other things. His mother, subscribing to the theory of "fresh air" therapy for disease recovery, had put my father in the backyard. There, a cardinal's song and springtime scents of damp earth and vague perfumes overwhelmed him. But when my father told this story, the power of those experiences only emerged in the shadow of his awareness of his own fragile health. Similarly, too, my father describes a trauma suffered a couple of years later that literally marked him for life:

> When I was eleven, I lost my right eye in a BB gun accident. It
> was just after the war and the guns were made of inferior metal

21

that sometimes jammed. Anyway, I can still remember every step in that terrible event. I walked down a country road carrying my BB gun to an old boat house on a lake I spent my summers at, Lake Waushakum in Sterling, Massachusetts. I was young and full of life, but of course also appropriately naïve and (some might say) reckless. I felt safe and secure. The idea of death or bodily harm seemed distant, if not impossible—certainly not a part of my consciousness. I crossed over a small brook that cut the road to enter the field behind the boathouse that jutted over the lake. As was my custom, I would shoot the gun at trees, rocks, or even (this now seems rather insensitive to me) at birds and small animals I would come across. Anyway, as I was standing in that field, a BB jammed in the gun and I needed to loosen the barrel of the gun to free it. Unfortunately, I did this by placing the butt of the gun on the ground and staring down the barrel. Of course, the gun fired a BB into my right eye. Fortunately the gun was not powerful enough to pierce my eye into my brain.

So at the age of eleven, my father was already scarred for life and clearly set apart from the others amongst whose lives he would have lost himself. Soon enough he passed through the door to adolescence, intensely aware of life's fragility. Whether set out there in his backyard or left for weeks in bed after the accident, my father couldn't just avoid the unpleasant possibility of immanent death. In his own consciousness, the question, "But will he survive?" must have been omnipresent.

Then, three summers after the BB-gun accident, something important happened. Here is how he wrote about that in one of his books, *Cosmology and Creation*:

> It was summer and I had just turned fourteen. My family and I spent our summers on Lake Waushakum in Sterling, Massachusetts. Sterling is north of Worcester. It remains a charming, small, typical central Massachusetts town with a short main street, a handful of stores, and a small central commons with a Civil War memorial in the middle. You take a right off Route 12 on Maple St. at the Town Hall, climb up a steep hill and follow a ridge for a mile or so till you come to the old Buttrick

farm and orchard. Taking another right leads you down through the orchard to a magnificent hill at its end overlooking the lake. It was here beneath an apple tree looking out over the lake that my summer-long experience began. It was an experience that changed me and how I saw life and my place within it.

The first time I experienced this sense of the wonder of existence was late afternoon, as the sun was beginning to set over the lake. The sky cloudless, and the lake reflected its high blue. I sat against one of the apple trees. The hay and wildflowers between the trees were high and the clover in the next field was in cheerful bloom. The sun was still warm on my arms and legs and I had to keep knocking horseflies off my arms before they inflicted their painful bites. There was a slight breeze that was cool on the back of my neck and stirred the apple boughs and grasses around me so that they seemed to whisper to one another like miserable old men. "What's he doing here? What's he doing here?"

I had been sitting for awhile not thinking of anything in particular, when I suddenly felt a rush of *wonder* at the spectacle before me. I don't mean "wonder" here in the sense of wondering about the solution to a problem or wondering how to solve a puzzle. There was nothing problem-solving—or for that matter hypothetical or even intellectual—about it. On the contrary, it was a feeling or mood of astonishment, a sense of how strange and weird life is as I contemplated the sheer existence of it all, including me. "How remarkable, how strange and surrealistic," I thought to myself, "that I am sitting here in these clothes (what are clothes?) on this hill redolent with incredible insects, butterflies, and numerous forms of vegetation, overlooking a lake (strange— what is that?) with something called the sun conveniently warming me while something else called a breeze cools me.

Integral to the question, "Would Paul Brockelman survive?" must be the implied follow-up: "If so, how?" He had already prepared the answer at nine in the redolent fragrance of his backyard: that he would live on by developing a strange sensitivity to the way his own fear of death might help him, might give him an advantage. His lakeside experience at

23

fourteen marked a decisive turn in this ongoing crisis of consciousness. Awareness of his own possible extinction marked a kind of unbearable anxiety standing right behind him, but now he began spinning the straw of such dread into the gold of a spiritual and poetic vision. By the lake, the natures of things pulsate with worry alongside my young father's own beating heart, against his fears that he might cease to be.

Repeated a thousand times over the course of his life, the success of my father's effort to weave his own risk into the fabric of reality actually helped him to survive and even to emerge from childhood: nothing like a purpose to transcend one's helplessness!

But what is "philosophical" about this? How did it lead my father to philosophy?

Paul Brockelman was the son of a German-American grocer and his wife, Estelle, who traced her heritage back to the *Mayflower* and the 17th-century English colonists settling in Massachusetts Bay. My father's stories pictured the family's life as uncannily resembling Norman Rockwell's covers from the old *Saturday Evening Post*—clear-cut if hackneyed character types and expectations, corny jokes, and narrowly fixed expectations. When McDonald's developed its formula for successful "fast food," with its emphasis on the fried and the familiar, they tested it in Worcester on people like the Brockelmans, who knew what they liked, and who didn't like anything new! As the inhabitants of Worcester understood it, this was not a place and the Brockelmans were not a family from which philosophers might spring. People there seemed entirely ensconced within provincial American life and the roles within it. My father said that life there just "seemed to make sense," with events and generations following each other in a natural order.

But my father's experience by the shores of Lake Waushakum forever cut him off from that "naturalness" and condemned him to a life of questioning natural orders. As he described his experience, a certain contingency in the way things are came to the forefront. Nothing necessitates even that I be here—wherever I am. Nor do the various things surrounding me ("clothes," "lakes," et cetera) have to be what they are. He describes it as a feeling that everything is "strange," "weird," even "surrealistic."

My father called the consciousness of such strangeness "philosophical."

Not that only philosophers have those experiences. My father's key assertion was that everybody has access to what he was talking about, albeit mostly unnoticed, unconscious access. Many religions view such contingency as precisely the phenomenon of "createdness" of things that testifies to the presence of divinity in the world. In a more philosophical and psychological perspective, the universality of my father's experience is simply traceable to the very form of human awareness that we call "self-consciousness." In having the thought that "I am aware of this" sits the notion that "this" could be otherwise.

In English, we think of "self-consciousness" as a negative trait, the paralyzing result of too much navel-gazing. Doing our utmost not to let consciousness paralyze us, we embrace the "normal" and "natural" ways of life into which we are born as ways of *escaping* the condition of a Hamlet, constantly overly aware of his own awareness. For my father, the philosopher was that person—allied with the theologian, but without the baggage—who refused to escape from over-awareness.

Plato and then Aristotle meant something like this when they announced that "philosophy begins in wonder." Philosophy emerges when we peel away a kind of socially imposed boredom, returning us to the way we would "first" find things without all the categories and connectors society forces upon us. Using the language that constitutes our shared experience can dry up the uniqueness and immediacy of living. One part of the path to philosophy for my father ran through the distrust he shared with thousands of years of philosophers over the way that social frameworks shape our reality.

His roots in "the tradition" ran deep. Book VII of *The Republic* is certainly one of the foundational texts for all of Western culture. Here, Plato's famous story about the education of philosophers—the "cave allegory"—begins from the unlikelihood that anybody might become a philosopher. By comparing the common human lot (with regard to knowledge) to imprisonment in a dark cave, Plato can frame the chances for philosophy as the probability of "seeing the light." The cave analogy, in fact, has us all chained up in a cave—so immobilized that we cannot turn our heads, forcing us to watch a kind of endless primitive television screen. This situation forces us to look only at the back wall of the cavern onto which the dim light of an otherwise hidden fire projects the shadows of puppets.

Moreover, a certain social, even political, pressure reinforces our collective fascination with the "show" to which life in the cave endlessly subjects us. Plato's narrator Socrates tells us that the prisoners "shout to one another," identifying the shadows on the wall and that they even hold "contests" and award honors to the most talented discerners of shapes from these shadows. In other words, society rewards adherence to its expectations for how to see things. The cave allegory also drives home that such pressure also works negatively, with the crowd teasing and finally even killing anybody who challenges the misidentification of the shadows as reality.

In the allegory of the cave, the philosopher's emergence depends upon others who free him from his chains and drag him into the light at the cave's entrance, where he gradually becomes able to discern the actual forms of the things for which, previously, he had only known shadows, themselves cast by mere outlines (the shadow puppets). Against his own will, this liberated prisoner eventually gains knowledge of both the things of which earlier he had had only the shadowiest understanding and, finally, of what allows any knowledge at all—the source of all light, the sun.

For Plato, being a philosopher means freeing oneself from the habits society imposes and the way of seeing things those habits bring with them. Plato's pessimism about the possibility that anybody might attain to philosophy without help may be related to the metaphor he gives us in the cave analogy for what makes someone a philosopher—light and the sun. Effectively, although everybody is born with the requisite faculties for philosophy—we have eyes to see the light—the "chains" of society keep most of us from ever having the experience that would lead us realize that potential.

My father certainly shared something with Plato and, through him, with at least half of the philosophy one meets in a Western University. He, too, believed that social structures and norms deeply shape how we see reality, and to that extent that we are all prisoners in such a cave. This was not a trivial debt to "the profession." I suspect that for all the effort and time he spent knocking what mainstream philosophy had become, my father's easy collegiality and sometime friendship with many other professional philosophers really has its source in a common platonic attitude: don't trust the way we generally talk about or even analyze our world! Much of what human beings daily take for granted and much of what we constantly reinforce in each other is an illusion, a way that we keep ourselves from facing a less comforting truth. That is a hidden faith of many philosophers, more in unconscious attitudes than in any actual creed —surprising in a group so dedicated to self-transparency.

But Paul Brockelman was not a Platonist, despite his commitment to the kind of social criticism that the story of "the cave" encourages. His identification with philosophy would have been complete and his professional integration uncontested, had he just shared the Platonist's faith in "the sun" that generates reality and provides knowledge to those who escape society's underground. My father's commitment to "experience" really meant that the source of all knowledge had to include the person formulating it. It can never be just something "out there," beyond us. Among other things, this means that we really can never "get used" to the experience of wonder in the way that the Platonist gets used to "the sun," transforming it (and all it illuminates) into an object of scientific study.

Because he challenged the language of an "objective" source of knowledge to describe where the philosopher looks for philosophy, he took exception to the "mainstream" of Western thought. The "wonder" he shared with other philosophers could never become what it easily was for them—a mere "wondering" addressed by scientific inquiry.

Instead, for my father the "strangeness" of the world revealed to the awestruck individual was *actually* how things were. It wasn't that some other "true" order appeared then, when the naturalness of normal ways of seeing faded away.

My father loved a rather strange film from the 1970s, made from that "Ripley's Believe It or Not" story, *The Enigma of Kaspar Hauser*. The story itself really belongs to the 19th-century equivalent of today's *National Enquirer* or to those "strange but true" links that appear at the bottom of internet webpages, though its basic events are well documented. One day in 1828, a teenaged boy showed up in Nuremberg, Germany, carrying a letter addressed to the local cavalry officer, giving his name and explaining his desire to be a "rider like my father before me." The young man himself seemed unable to speak and only later (after much education) told a story of having been raised entirely within a darkened room without any exposure to the outside world or to other human beings, a kind of wildling.

In the film version of Kaspar Hauser that my father knew, made by the mystical and controversial Werner Herzog, the experience of being awestruck is in fact chronologically first—a convenient fact that is usually not the case in the stories we tell about our lives. Here the "most important" or "foundational" experience actually does begin things. Wonder is Kaspar's earliest (and thus formative) real experience of the world. It is the moment when the mysterious agent manipulating his fate pulls him out of the dark room where, eyes deprived of all light, mind deprived of all society and with it of all conversation and even language, Kaspar has been forced to spend his entire childhood. So, his captor drags Kaspar out the door of that dark tower, his home and prison, into a Nuremberg summer's day.

In the film, because he stumbles from "nothing" to a sudden "everything," the moment overwhelms Kaspar Hauser. With neither his senses dulled by constant use, his imagination lulled by comparison to other experiences, nor his awareness blunted by habituation, the experience of something so simple as a "view," a "field," can shock the mind and body. There kneels Kaspar, dumbstruck by the wonder of his first summer day and, in the filmmaker's hands, the moment overtakes us, too. Oversaturated with '70s Technicolor and accompanied by a score of Renaissance polyphonic choral music, Herzog's film sweeps its audience up at its first communal sight of that day overwhelming Kaspar Hauser. It's just a movie and viewing it only evokes a shadow of what my father directly experienced by Lake Waushakum, but seeing Kaspar's *first* experience helps us to understand why my father took that day by the lake to hold the primary truth about his life, a sense of "first-timeness" that never grew old for him.

And the point about this kind of wonder, before which Kaspar falls to the ground and my father's jaw drops open, is that an ocean separates it from the "wondering" of scientists and philosophers about just how things work or don't. Because it directs itself at "me" as much as at the world, wonder is out of control, bowel-loosening, transformative—not pleasant, musing, and methodical. We are closer to God speaking from burning bushes than to the lab! This might be why, despite his profound apostasy, my father always felt most at home when pursuing religious matters. More than the philosopher at least, the religious person understood the irreducibility of awe and even fear.

Even if you have never formally studied philosophy, I bet that you will understand how much of a rebel my father was. Isn't philosophy all about the mind, sort of an ethics of science? For that basic idea, my father held a life-sustaining disdain! For him, nobody could justly reduce that sense of newness and mystery accompanying his own experience to "science." Especially Plato profoundly misunderstood it, when he pushed it toward some potential knowledge. Wonder, for my father, happens when we let go, when we stop trying to come up with a scientific explanation for the world. The purpose of his work was to underscore the awful importance of the mind's fearless passage beyond what it could comprehend rationally.

Embarrassingly but genuinely, my father had one idea and only one—this one about wonder. I call him a philosopher because his entire life unfolded from that idea, and his long adventure demanded judgment by his fidelity to it. When his life faltered, it did so because he mistook the demands of that idea or somehow failed to live up to them. But he knew the contract he had signed. And his idea came from this one experience, this one story.

Paul Brockelman's path to philosophy lay just there, where radical wonder crossed his distrust of the "everyday" fashion in which society and habit form our seeing. Above all, what made him a philosopher was his insistence on placing himself in the midst of mystery, even though he was aware of how the structures of life unavoidably divert that stream. Aware that all the forces of "normal life" conspire to deaden us, he called attention to the endlessly open realm of existence out beyond the narrow cone of light cast by the familiar. He knew that none of us could really claim to "live out there." Nevertheless, he insisted that, ever anew, we break the spell of the everyday in favor of the extraordinary that he knew lurked at its boundaries.

MEDITATION 2 REBELS WITHOUT AND WITH CAUSES

What should I do with my life? What is my vocation?

1.   Tom Donahue, my grandfather on my mother's side, lived an interesting life. He wasn't really my grandfather at all. My grandmother Sylvia's early marriage in the Bronx to an Algerian man (that he shared her Jewish background made him acceptable if still unusual to her Viennese family) had broken up quickly, leaving an increasingly unstable young woman of still marriageable age with a daughter. Into that picture walked young Tom, the handsome but uneducated youngest of an Irish Catholic family freshly off the boat from County Kerry. But Tom's biggest plus, though he was strikingly handsome, was his interest in marrying my grandmother. It would have been obvious that Sylvia Davis was a bit crazy from early on. She had episodes of "nerves" even as a young woman. Still, she had a bit of money, more than the Donahues ever did, enough that the price of a merely theoretical future loyalty from the youthful "ladies' man" made sense.

    That doesn't mean that things in the new Donahue family were idyllic, however. My mother hated Tom Donahue with a passion only equaled by the venom she reserved for *her* mother. She claimed Tom was the original model for Archie Bunker of *All in the Family*, combining ignorance, pig-headed opinions, and low-level corruption. He certainly shared Archie Bunker's tendency to malapropism—often ordering "condominiums" to accompany a meal and loudly declaiming about the "electrical college" in presidential election years. Sylvia had to be institutionalized at least a couple of times over the years, so she can't have been an easy partner. Still, some combination of self-interest and loyalty kept Tom with my grandmother for more than forty years.

I mention this stability in Tom's life because it contrasted markedly with something else about him. The most consistent description of Tom's career was that he was a "driver." Over the course of his life, this title covered various odd jobs from loading dock work, to driving tractor-trailers, to teaching truck-driving in New Jersey, to courier package-delivery. Rumors of his adventures in trucking included mob connections (he writes about a time that he and some "fellows" threatened to unload an order of produce in the middle of the George Washington Bridge at rush hour) and a stint working for the unsavory Dominican dictator, Rafael Trujillo. Whatever the truth of such tales—always difficult to separate from the fiction of his life— Tom Donahue enjoyed a long series of jobs in the trucking industry. Many paid him very well—well enough so that he and my grandmother could purchase a penthouse apartment in Riverdale—and kept him busy well into old age.

But he certainly never had a "calling." In his various relationships to them over the years, trucks were various means to the singular end of supporting himself and my grandmother. Trucking was a lucrative "profession" that he pursued just so far and so long as he had to. Driving simply provided Tom the launch pad for many of his picaresque adventures, from his youthful "jobs" for the local produce industry to his "glamorous" chauffeuring of Andre Kostelanetz and other NBC radio stars. As he himself explained to me, it got Tom out in the world. End of story.

As was typical for the 1930s and 1940s, Paul Brockelman's parents expected him to take over his family's business, a chain of grocery stores in and around Worcester, Massachusetts. In fact, Dad was only the second son. His older brother Henry was so extremely introverted (probably a form of autism) that my father, who always got along with people, was the natural choice for the job. Bernard and Estelle Brockelman's marriage combined the Taylors, an Anglo-American family with roots reaching back to the Pilgrims, and the Brockelmans, a more recent German immigrant branch. Their union fit perfectly in the "American Dream" pattern of immigrant assimilation and social climbing and granted Bernard's Germanic business skill a patina of social acceptability. The road ahead seemed well paved for their younger son. Business and wealth accumulation would allow my father some combination of comfort and responsibility. Except that he wouldn't go that way.

In *Seeing Life Whole Again*, my father relates this discovery of his while in high school, working for his father in one of the family's grocery stores:

> It was the Worcester Market, one of the largest grocery stores in New England (yes, I was proud of my father). I was working on the fruit counter toward the front of the store, a rectangular counter about fifty by one hundred feet piled high with various kinds of fruit. I didn't like working there. For some reason, I didn't enjoy waiting on customers, not because I was above them, but because it just seemed like the same old thing over and over and over. In other words, it was boring! I did enjoy carefully arranging the great mounds of fruit for display, but, alas, any sales of that fruit immediately destroyed the aesthetic order I had so carefully contrived. In fact, the routines of selling fruit seemed boring to me.

And so my father would grab one of those oranges whose sale so put him to sleep and head to the woods, there to read Will Durant's *Story of Philosophy*. He explains that it wasn't anything specific about Durant's account or the many philosophers Durant writes about that fascinated him. Rather, it was the reflective mood that the writer demanded from his reader and that one particular young reader was overjoyed to provide. As my father puts it:

> I loved losing myself in the text, I loved the peace and quiet; but most of all I loved feeling in touch with life by being conscious of it! I loved being mindful, even if it was only for an hour or so break between my tasks at the market. I loved paying attention to life rather than hurrying to accomplish this or that task.

Together, this quiet introduction into philosophical reflection versus the "accomplishment of tasks" and the transforming experience by Lake Waushakum pushed my father to a different *idea* of what kind of career he might pursue—to something closer to a vocation or a calling.

Of course, my father's choice to search for "meaning" in his career was also an identifiable American pattern: parents who had "made it" to the middle classes and given their son every opportunity to succeed (Philips Andover, Dartmouth) watched in horror as he discovered poetry, religion (seriously contemplating ministry), and finally philosophy. We all know the peculiar challenge such life choices represent: it's not just that the life poetic seems impractical—low paying, low success—but, more significantly, the "payoff" is incomprehensible within the contours of a narrowly defined "American Dream," where each generation's task is to visibly improve the family's material lot. As they saw it, choosing relative poverty and social invisibility instead almost amounted to an insult to his parents. They seemed to ask, "What did we do wrong?" or "Why do you hate us?" It took a particular kind of courage, which in their own way my parents found together, to make it. This path of the prodigal son is well worn in human history, and my father walked it, deeply convinced of the value of what he was doing.

2. I grew up intensely aware of how those who *did* enjoy a vocation were different than those who did not, whether that difference was the cause of their career choices or a result of them. Every Thanksgiving, every Christmas, over the supposedly festive table, two generations in my family fought a long, pitched battle over contrasting ways to think about a good life. The 1960s provided ample fertile ground for conflict between my parents and their parents. But in my extended family, the question of vocation focused my parents on the meaningfulness of what they *did* and both sets of grandparents on what they *had*.

The nature of this war determined the sides, allying my mother's working class, urban family and my father's "waspy," cloth-coat Republican family—people who wouldn't otherwise necessarily agree about much— against those weird, pointy headed academic types, my parents. So those were the opposing teams for my entire childhood and youth.

Visits to or from any of the grandparents almost inevitably led to tension and mutual recrimination, so that my mother would get stress headaches days before the actual event. She inevitably planned to minimize intergenerational contact, including accommodations for the grandparents in a local hotel. In the mid-1960s, the moment of the much discussed "generation gap," my parents were hardly alone in their alienation from their parents; we all know the complex ways that this generational split played out in America's culture and politics. For my father, setting up the tents for a new American way of life and fighting the battles for its birth—civil rights, Vietnam, and with a good shove from my mother, the women's movement—

absorbed his energies entirely until, with grown kids, he faced midlife in a changed America.

In my family, "Vietnam and all of that" mostly offered a pretext for a struggle that predated the politics of the day. Really, they fought over the bewilderment and resentment my grandparents' generation felt about the choices my parents had made: why wasn't the life that my grandparents had lived "good enough"? What was wrong with the perfectly decent, successful paths they had taken? After all, American society rewarded their choices, making my father's parents pillars of social responsibility in suburban Massachusetts and allowing my mother's parents, Tom and Sylvia, to winter each year in Florida.

To all appearances, though, the unfolding vision of a different and new America, one eschewing militarism and proudly including those barred from the older America (women, African Americans, gays) tended to set our holiday fights ablaze. Indeed, both of my parents gave plenty of incitement. My father's embrace of "the movement" was public and famous. He became the faculty liaison at the University of New Hampshire to the local chapter of the SDS (Students for a Democratic Society), an organization of agitators whose more radical, West Coast chapters embraced "violent resistance" and whose local representatives pulled him to the head of several angry marches in 1967 and 68. In the atmosphere of the day, the older generation could not ignore such a provocation, nor could they resist treating my father's protests as some kind of nuttiness. It was generally agreed that my father had too much time on his hands and would be better off with a "real" job.

3. We most typically apply the language of vocation to paths of the religious—to the choice, say within a Christian church, to become a minister, priest, or nun. There, I suppose, the notion is that God has literally "called" someone to make a commitment that would span an entire lifetime. Even to those of us for whom this language seems strange or even hostile, it's still possible to import something of the resonance of the religious calling, to speak of a vocation as a choice of one's "life work." If you think about it, any time that any of us make such life-choices, we assert two things— both that the direction captures some essential element of my character (or what I take to be my character) and that, as an activity or a world of tasks, it contains the capacity to grow and change as I do. A calling or vocation lasts a lifetime! This suggests that one has chosen a "field" broad enough and deep enough to support a lifetime of individual growth: screwing on the toothpaste cap, which Roald Dahl chose for Charlie's father in *Charlie and the Chocolate Factory*, "calls" nobody, though it may offer a decent job to somebody for a while.

Behind this lies an idea that pops up at key moments as the modern world emerges, namely, that *work* can play a key role in making us who we are. We aren't just born with a character, we create one and we do so, at least in part, through the work that we accomplish. If such self-creating labor has a single purpose over the long haul, we might name it a "calling." Hopefully, you have known somebody who can speak in this way of "their work" and what its formation and completion demand—a judge, an artist, a violin-maker. Or a philosopher.

No less shocking an intellectual than Karl Marx ran a good way with the ball here. Like much else in the German philosopher's work, his intentions are cloudy. But one could still make a convincing case that at least amongst the younger Marx's purposes (up through 1848) lay the idea that such vocation was central to human self-realization—to living a life that felt genuinely satisfying, genuinely human—so that an end or purpose of the Communist revolution was a society in which *everybody* would have their "own" work. That is, the opportunities of character formation and growth that we attach to a "calling" were not limited to any privileged few lucky enough to afford such a thing.

Both Marx and his philosophical predecessors, Friedrich Schiller and Georg Wilhelm Friedrich Hegel, saw that this conception of work should be more than the preserve of a lucky few. We still possess a video of my daughter at two years old, playing the game she called "my little office." This was her best approximation of adulthood, complete with meaningless piles of paper to sort through and various miniature objects to re-arrange. Copying her academic parents, she was trying to play into the world of work she observed around her.

Or think of the six-year-old boy who runs around his house dressed in a fireman's hat and overcoat, perhaps adding, to his parents' annoyance, a simulated wailing of sirens: he is pretending, trying on an identity, because that's part of "growing up." That child might or might not really be cut out for the work of fire abatement but thinking of himself that way for a little while will influence how he sees himself. We don't just "discover" who we are. We create that identity—in part through increasingly serious play with a range of possible professions. Because he played so seriously at it, that kid will grow up to be, at least a little bit, a fireman. Maybe, he'll want to be a hero or just identify with those who put themselves in harm's way to help others. Whatever the exact incorporation of any given identification, the point is that each contributes to shaping who "I" am.

The point is not just that we play at working (although we do) but that such play is *already* a kind of pre-work—the labor of trying on a character. Like trying on clothes, it's a way of both judging the vest or coat and judging *myself*; how do *I* look in *that*?

That kind of play that both creates and endlessly transforms identity can continue through a life, if one is lucky enough to possess a sense of vocation. My father would "work on" his papers and books, even when nobody else cared that he did—on vacation, when he needed more sleep, and in the very last year when he knew that he could no longer really participate in the scholarly discussion that had always before been one product of his labors. He continued that work long after he knew pretty much who he was—long past being a child first discovering himself.

4. Paul Brockelman, of course, didn't spend his life playing fireman. He spent it joyously repeating the gestures of the philosopher. In "mindfulness," in the quiet spaces of reading and writing, he somehow touched the experience of wonder that he first knew by the shores of Lake Waushakum. No doubt ingredient to this work were his hours spent in front of young students, his efforts to found new directions in education, the public talks and lectures. But the core of his work took place alone, in the moments when he could pull back from active engagement with the world, to experience something of the openness, the infinite horizon of possibility, that he associated with the experience of mystery. Life was more than this or that project, this or that person, and the great therapy for him of the philosopher's calling was that it endlessly reminded him of that.

Along with the childhood case of the measles that likely caused his eventual deafness, my father's teenage BB gun accident had consequences to the end of his life. In his early sixties, my father's growing difficulty in hearing his students in the classroom hastened his retirement from teaching. No doubt the isolation of deafness was painful. I love to tell the way that my father kept his sense of humor, or at least cheerfulness, until the end, joking about himself as a cyborg with his glass eye, plastic hip, and metal shoulder. Truth is, though, that you can't really be funny if you can't hear. My father's humor had always been of the story telling variety. But as hearing failed him, he discovered how much every story teller depends on cues from his audience. So the story of the time when Dad and his crazy painter friend, Dirk, desperate for something to smoke back in the 60s, tried banana peels—no high but a powerful stink! —became boring when his deafness made him oblivious to our mood.

Still, he had his work. Even if I prefer to remember my father as a great teacher, he was also a writer, and he wrote his most powerful and successful book, *Cosmology and Creation*, after his retirement but before he became really elderly. Writing philosophy became a consolation for him in those years when the encroachment of both his and my mother's deaths became unmistakable. In such a time, his vocation was worth treasuring for what meaning and order it could deliver in an otherwise anxious life. And, in truth, my father could comfort himself that his work still produced something worthwhile, long after his forced retreat from the pleasant classrooms of his younger years.

Alas, loss of sight eventually also tore up the virtuous contract behind my father's writing. With only one good eye, he was defenseless against common afflictions late in life. When his sight in that eye began to degenerate rapidly in his sixties, he took the advice of a conservative opthalmologist and refused the risk of an operation, accepting encroaching blindness for many years. It wasn't until he moved to Syracuse after my mother's death that we convinced him to get another opinion and try the procedure. Years of scarring and degeneration limited his recovered sight. With the onset of glaucoma, my father's visual walls closed in further. Even reading, the easy path for his insatiable curiosity for most of his life, became increasingly difficult.

As he was able to read less and less, my father's world closed down in a rather obvious way. His was an inevitable downward slope leading from blindness to a shortening attention span to, in the end, the full old fogey's life, with the droning TV constantly in the background. At the very least, my father knew what real scholarship was, and he knew that if he could not read lengthy or difficult texts anymore, he couldn't do it. And that depressed him.

Still, such was the power of his vocation that my father never ceased to play at it. As the manuscript of *Seeing Life Whole Again* attests, he got up in the morning, sat down at the computer, and continued the story. We all know such an opportunity to work when one no longer needs to is a luxury, a by-product of a stable and affluent society. In an era when ever fewer people can enjoy access to such a genuine calling, one that staves off the paralyzing fear of death far into old age, I mourn both my father's profession and the easy ideal of a world where more people could have "work" in the way that he did. In acknowledging the reality that today's students may switch both jobs and careers four or five times during their lives, we educators often give up creating the vision of vocation at all. Instead, we liken the person to a tool kit and train them for flexibility above all. Something is lost there.

Maybe that doesn't have to be the case, even if the easy paths to professorships or similar life-long careers have mostly disappeared. Maybe we can educate young people to play at being themselves even without those easy institutional supports. No matter how hard to achieve, such a goal becomes even more important as modernity speeds up change, melting "all that is solid into air." A world in which ever-accelerating transformation is the rule demands the steadiness that only a vocation like Paul Brockelman's can give to a life.

MEDITATION 3 PAUL'S BIG LOVE

What is love?

One testimony to my father's extraordinary character is his choice of my mother. Few sons of Worcester's middle class would have had the courage to woo Barbara Davis, dark Jewish artist from the Bronx! She wasn't just exotic. She was also passionately engaged in everything strange to young Paul—jazz, Leftist politics, European fashion, and, above all, the art scene. Such an array of passions and the fact that they *were* passions, separated my mother from the suburban women with their mild "interests" and projects and reasonable expectations whom he was supposed to consider.

But even that word, "passions" fails to describe Barbara's loves. When my mother devoted herself to something or someone, she made a total commitment. Her faith in that thing or person was complete, and she granted an undivided commitment. She knew no doubt. Perhaps this undividedness was Barbara's dominant trait. When she took on a cause (and there were always at least a couple at any moment) she became a force of nature for whatever it was. Because she so completely believed, her energy and resolve would transform people and projects, moving them forward in a way that had earlier seemed unlikely. Of course, the same undividedness in her character birthed her hatreds as well as her loves. My mother was a great hater, and there was always the danger that even her passion for my father might "go over to the dark side." This never happened. Even in their most consuming battles, my parents' love never went through the strange barometric inversion that occurred when my mother lost faith in her other causes. This testifies to something extraordinary between them, deeper than I can analyze.

It has taken me many years to understand just how unusual the love between my father and my mother was. It *was* a big love: you almost wanted to add, "TM," so unique was their "brand." Many more people in the New Hampshire Seacoast area knew "Barbara and Paul" than knew either of them individually, and when my mother died, so did many of these "salon friendships" that really only existed with the pair of them. Those friends seemed almost to sink into the ground, leaving only my father's more modest group. At times in their fifty-five years together, that collective "Paul and Barbara" marked something more like a mobile space than it did a mere relationship, a place you could go for discussion and debate of the hot intellectual and political topics of the day or just for a meal with good company.

This dedication of a space defined my world as a child, too. My own experience of my parents' relationship came mostly in its seemingly effortless consecration of a place, the family in which I grew up. Together they were the home extending beyond any house, the security that allowed my sister and me to explore the world with maximum trust and freedom. Boundaries existed, times and places when each or both of them would reel us in from our wandering dives into the unknown, but they were broad and generous. Really, knowing of those limits contributed to our freedom rather than contesting it.

At five, my early enthusiasm for kindergarten led me one day to bike the two or three miles to school an hour before it started. Smitten with my appropriately named teacher, Mrs. Valentine, I had braved distance to be alone with her! Alarmed, she called home, resulting in a lecture from my father about the dangers of disappearing, something that I should "never do again!" But I still remember the pleased grin while he delivered this sermon every bit as much as his rebuke. Clearly, the way that our home gave me self-confidence pleased him as much as my pilgrimage disturbed him. My parents' love alone gave me the strength to wander so far on such a forbidden journey.

This reassurance helped both of them, too. As his son, I witnessed several of my father's worst moments, the moments when anxiety most thoroughly consumed him: in 1972, when the political backlash from the 1960s came in the form of vendettas from his colleagues and the University

Wedding Photo: Barbara & Paul Brockelman, 1958

administration, in the aftermath of an affair around that same time that almost blew up his marriage, and when my mother faced the death to which a lifelong inability to stop smoking had condemned her. But while I knew my father in doubt and grief, those moments always occurred against the backdrop of something else: the thing that was so manifest in the good, clear life my mother and he constructed together. We all *knew* that other thing, "Paul and Barbara," in our bones, and it calmed us, not least my father.

One reliable index of the value of their big love was how difficult it must have been to conceive, never mind to realize. Even though my father was an oddity, a self-exile from his waspy-Worcester-world, the very idea of Barbara Davis should have been unimaginable to him. The resistance to the match of both families reinforces that fact. To begin with, the couple's very meeting was unlikely. My father's family shipped him off for a long summer working on Madison Avenue in one of those "Madmen" firms where he met my mother, then a secretary and love interest of the firm's rising young star. That my father won her away from Marvin Gardner was immortalized to my ears by years of laments from my grandmother, Sylvia, who muttered disbelievingly for the rest of her life, "Why did she prefer this goy to the man who managed the Volvo account?"

It's a bit difficult to describe my father in his relationship with my mother because she was the dominant one, the one whose voice spoke for "them." This did change considerably over the years. In the early years, my father's personality was relatively strong. His brilliance and energy were at their greatest in the 1960s and 70s, when social and political upheaval kept the teaching of an open and creative philosopher in the eyes of thousands of New Hampshire college students. As my father entered his fifties, a series of heart attacks crippled him, collectively "knocking the stuffing out of him." At the same time, a career as a psychotherapist brought my mother into her own. Beginning as a mere secretary in a university student counseling office, she was soon seeing clients and setting off on a successful career as a feminist therapist. While my mother's energy expanded, my father's shrank, and, of course, his sight and hearing were increasing blocks to easy sociability.

Regardless, she was always top dog, even when I was a kid. When they fought, which they did often and loudly, it was her voice—her screams, sobs, and even throwing of ashtrays—that we heard. My father always answered "rationally," his deep voice audible but the words indistinct from the other room where my sister and I inevitably listened. Occasionally, we'd hear his deep teacher's voice deliver, "But Barbara, that's just not true." Or, "Shouldn't I have a say here, too?" But not only did her fury lead, it also paced my father. We always knew when the fight was nearing its end because then alone would he abandon that "reasoned" tone, his voice rising to a shrill falsetto as he would scream, "I just can't take it anymore!"

Then things would go quiet, with only occasional mutual sobs breaking the sound barrier between rooms. Eventually they would emerge, hand in hand, to announce some new state of things. She had won again, as she always did with him—breaking through his intellectual reserve to an admission of whatever feelings underlay her anger.

This was what bound him to her—this debt to the realm of feelings for which his family had failed to prepare him. Somehow, he needed to acknowledge that region in order to grow, to realize the philosophical vision of Lake Waushakum. For what would such a philosopher be, a thinker of experience, an enemy of Plato's pure rationalism, who could not walk the corridors of emotion? If my father was to defend an experience beyond science, then he needed what my mother offered him. And he knew it, too, sometimes engaging in an exaggerated self-abasement after their arguments ("Oh, I am *such* an idiot!").

Of course, she also needed him! While she was never as good at acknowledging it, he gave her life structure, form—a stability that, for most of her life, contained the "crazy" that re-surfaced from her mother sometimes, threatening to consume her.

It's often difficult to see the difference one person makes in another's life, the way that a love transforms each life it touches. I've already mentioned how unimaginable my mother was in Worcester, Massachusetts, in the 1950s. While a "night out" for the Brockelmans always involved Howard Johnsons—the perfect "cloth coat Republican" venue for the comfortably middle-class wanting to demonstrate their social superiority to fast food without actually abandoning the burger and the frier—my mother's skills as a French chef allowed her to create occasional meals at the top restaurants in New Hampshire. From college onward, my returns home always involved some elaborate concoction, usually with experimental new flavors. "No fuss," she'd say, as she brought the perfect cheese soufflé to the table, "Just something I put together after work."

My father went along with all of this, gamely trying most things and retreating without complaint afterwards to the dish sink where he'd clean up the devastation. Salads seemed to be his limit—he'd refuse more than symbolic quantities of the newest healthy greens. In the last two or three years of her life, we knew that Mom was approaching a real crisis when this theatrical gesture of joyful, miraculous cookery failed her and she'd ask me to make dinner. And the glory of my mother's kitchen wasn't only for me,

49

my friends and girlfriends, or eventually my own wife and family. Dinners at Barbara and Paul's were legendary, the location of their ever-widening circle from the artists, feminist therapists, or philosophers with whom each created attachments. So, for over forty years my mother and father formed that remarkable community known everywhere along the Seacoast as "Barbara and Paul's Friends."

The point of all of this is that the life of the table marks the clearest place to measure the difference that my mother made in my father's life. After she died, my father erected what amounted to an informal protest against more than five decades of gourmet eating, even in the face of doctors' warning against this, insisting on an almost exclusive diet of burgers and fries. Any burger that arrived at the table with even a leaf of lettuce he summarily returned to the kitchen for defoliation. No salads! In fact, nothing green. In fact, no more fancy meals at all. I wasn't going to deny my father the right to eat like a rube, even if it killed him! But I wondered how his culinary rebellion marked a broader battle against my mother's influence. He hadn't really needed her: he could just let her go!

But no matter how stubbornly rebellious, my father's message of independence from my mother was off. He needed her, or more precisely, he had needed her. Perhaps, by the time she died, she had already largely played her role. Even his symbolic rebellion was remarkably circumscribed: after we sold the big farmhouse in Eliot, Maine, where they spent the final years of their marriage and where my mother died, my father surrounded himself with reminders of her—the many works of art, some painted by her and some by their friends, the strange combination of modernist design sensibility in furniture and fixtures with an almost Victorian sense of pattern and bold color that my mother had loved, even her best French cooking pots and pans. In those last years, after he had moved to Syracuse, my father confessed to me how naïve he'd been before he met her—as close to a confession that she'd changed him as he could make. My mother opened my father's eyes to the world—to art and music and political intensity and above all to the beauty of complexity and ambiguity. Even in the blindness of his last years, he wasn't going to close them again to any of that.

Plato's great dialogue about erotic love, the Symposium, contains two speeches that, together, shed light on the story of my father's big love. The first is an interlude by Aristophanes, 5th-Century Athens' great comic playwright. Here, Aristophanes drops the metaphor that many of us still use when describing the search for love as seeking your "other half." In Plato's dialogue, Aristophanes tells the story of how Zeus fated human beings to look for that other side of themselves as though for the reverse side of a coin. Finding this complement to one's self is the key to a sense of completion and human fulfillment: "Each of us when separated, having one side only, like a flat fish, is but the tally-half of a man, and he is always looking for his other half."

I saw enough of the pain resulting from my parents' long marriage to criticize it thoroughly, even to wonder why my mother stayed with my father through several flirtations with female students or why he stayed with her through long years when she fought with depression and madness. Because my parents seemed to "complete" each other from adulthood on—each to provide the "missing piece" to the other—I never really took seriously the possibility that they could separate. I guess the same dynamic seemed to count for them; like it or not (and both of them did sometimes dislike it), they were bound together for the duration!

Socrates himself delivers the other, and far greater, speech in The Symposium, but in a peculiar indirect language that supposedly recounts an earlier story told him by "Diotima," a priestess of Mantis. One of the most important documents of Western philosophy, this speech is valuable for multiple reasons, but one aspect in particular speaks deeply of my parents' relationship. The so-called "ladder" of different kinds of love, much of the speech, makes an extended argument for the *fruitfulness* of love. When we love, we find something beautiful and pursue that beauty, in order to give birth to something beyond our individual, mortal lives. When love reaches its highest level—the desire for beauty per se— Diotima and Socrates equate the immortal something that they hope to establish with "the Good" itself—a key part of the Socratic and Platonic vision. No matter the level, though, love generates something beyond either of the lovers, something more enduring and important than either of them as individuals.

The love letters between my parents that have surfaced recently reveal that they surely knew from very early on that this was "the big one" for them, that this love was the moment when both sensed the presence of something bigger than either of them individually. My sister, Mira, and I knew well the physical passion that underlay Dad and Mom's big love: they were easily and extraordinarily in love for much of their lives. But the letters reveal that their occasional horseplay ("Pauly," my mother would taunt, "you wouldn't tickle me, would you?"), only grew alongside this more serious sense: in one letter, Paul oscillates between rather hot expressions of desire and insistence that he cannot see her for the next month because he needs to complete his graduate school applications. "Barbara, dearest," he writes, "you know that the life we both want can only happen if we spend these weeks apart."

A life vision like that is, I think, an "offspring" deserving ambivalence—one that is both precious and difficult. It threatens, strangely, to overwhelm its parents, to submerge the individual talents of both father and mother in its support. "Barbara and Paul" was a greater good, a more immortal offspring, than either of my parents could ever produce alone. This was the good origin of the "Great Seacoast Salon," of their ability to found a home for a whole community, including themselves. But the problem with the fruit of such a relationship is that is produces obligation, even when the lovers, individually, would rather live unbound. Afterward, nobody that such a love touches is ever really free from it.

That sense of being obliged explains the passion and even violence of those many fights between them. Each knew that they were bound to the relationship, even when each individually might have preferred just to go on to someone or something else. Mira and I, their children, have also felt the weight of this greater good as obliging us, too, like some greedy third sibling: we both have felt we must continue the vision that "Barbara and Paul" brought into being. I can only imagine the ambivalence that our parents felt as they carried this ideal child about.

Those who knew and loved my parents are dying off. The great Seacoast Salon is a fading memory. When I was younger, I imagined that I would someday found my own love with somebody at the scale of the one between Mom and Dad. But now I see that their relationship, sealed in youthful passion and polished through all the disruptions of mid-life and aging, was a piece with the lifelong commitment that marked their entire journey. Not every human life can bear an immortal love because not every life can create a way of life! Having discovered a wonderful companion in my late thirties, a companion with whom I have raised a daughter and shared twenty-five years of my life, I don't discount my own contribution to the table of love! However, to accept that such an offering is somehow smaller, further from "the Good" that Diotima, Socrates, and Plato envision, is neither self-flagellation nor excessive praise of my parents: it is simply that I accept the rarity and value of what they had.

Perhaps I am writing now to try my own meager talents in at least preserving that "big love," a love that, like the one in *The Symposium* itself, could live beyond them or me. I feel entirely unfit for such a task and console myself by thinking that the love between my father and my mother lives on in many other ways—in the lives and projects they nourished. However, one thing I have learned in middle age—I think I may be more aware of this than either of them—is that one of the true payoffs of what my father called "wonder," wherever we find it, is thankfulness. To wonder genuinely at a day, a person or, in this case, a relationship, is to experience profound gratitude about it, to have a love to give back for the love received. My justification, no, my invocation for a text on Dad's "big love" would be my thank-offering for it.

MEDITATION 4 THE BROKEN CONVERSATION

Must philosophy be a dialogue?

It's true that, as a young man, my father fled Worcester, Massachusetts, and the career in business waiting for him there. But that flight shouldn't give you the idea that he was inept with people. Quite the contrary. The lifelong irony was his gift for the "schmoozing" part of social life necessary to succeed in business. As far back as I can remember and until the end of his life, anybody who visited my family was likely to get the full "Paul Brockelman Show" treatment. That's what we called his tendency to "interview" "guests"—kids' friends, dishwasher repairmen, you name it! —as though on television. The set-up for the interview was my father's intense focus upon and interest in their lives. "How did you get interested in dishwashers? What drew you to the repairman's business? How does your job fit into your beliefs about what makes life worth living?" "What matters to you?"

The questions were fairly predictable. Mostly these interactions worked; few indeed were the people who didn't open up even a little bit. My father could give almost anybody a sense that they were a special person, that their story was intensely interesting, that it was worth taking his time out of a busy day or evening to discuss that person's life. You might doubt this success: I know my father sounds, well, a bit obnoxious. But somehow the interview always followed—however immediately— some exchange of empathy, some establishment of human contact that caused his "interviewees" to grant him unspoken permission for his cross-examination. So his questions never came off as heckling or badgering because they always arose in the context of somebody *just* realizing that "they liked this guy, Paul Brockelman."

The connection my father established with such guests was authentic: "That Jim Dodge," my father would later mention about the repairman, "He's a really courageous guy. Did you know that he's been guiding his family through his mother's cancer?" Only such authentic and reciprocal connection could explain the universal acceptance of my father's inconvenient probing. But in *that* context people just took it as a key experience of their new friend.

I fell in love with my father's philosophical schmoozing early and hard. Nothing fascinated me more than the relaxed yet intense flow of time during one of his "interviews," and I would listen for hours. I remember at eight or nine eavesdropping on a discussion from a hiding place under a wicker chair between my father and one of his students. Of course, my father and his student, Allie, knew full well that I was there, but they let me maintain my illusion of secrecy, excusing me from having to answer embarrassing questions about my interest in adult conversation. Though "safe" in my cozy invisibility, I was thrilled by the drama of the philosophical story and already effectively lost to any life that didn't involve lots of this kind of thing!

When my father died, we held an initial memorial service for him at the small Jesuit College where I work. The surprisingly hefty attendance at this event included a considerable number of "interviewees" from my father's very last years in Syracuse—his personal trainer from the local gym, his hearing aid technician, his nurse's aide—all in addition to the family of Louise (not her real name), the woman with whom he had fallen in love at the end. All came to mourn my father because all had shared some moment of philosophical connection with him—that is, his remarkable ability to converse.

I never ceased to marvel at my father's capacity to open a spontaneous new segment of "The Paul Brockelman Show" —anytime, anyplace. The interview always began with a question like, "So, for you, what is the meaning of life?" This was precisely my mother's signal for annoyance and a diversion. She feared that the art patron who had come to view paintings, or the friend meant to comfort her for some loss, might never do what they had come to do. As my father drew into old age and he could only hear with difficulty, it's true that the interviews involved less genuine delving into the other person's story and more lecturing about what he thought. None of this destroyed the sense of connection that was the foundation of my father's probing.

Only in middle age did I discover in myself something of my father's talent for connection. Though I'll never approach his ability to engage anyone, anytime, a period helping my college out as an administrator revealed to me that I, too, could schmooze. Beyond the fact that I, famous misanthrope, could actually enjoy easy companionship—that I could like *people*—I had never suspected what this could add to my ability as a philosopher.

Somehow, I had just never put together that my *own* talent for philosophising with others already contained this instinct for human connection. To have that interest in just *how* Joe or Jill or Farhid is doing— how his kids are or what she thinks is true about the world—is to discover a *common humanity* emotionally with a specific other. Schmoozing springs from this sense of shared human value—a sense of equality in being human. Without that, no philosophy ensues.

Dad was a good, if sometimes indulgent father. Certainly his sympathy with others, no matter how different they might be, that ability to discover common humanity, made him so. Despite his solemn, bearded face, neither my sister nor I found our father intimidating. We admired him for his quiet wisdom when he listened even to us and his determination to take as much pleasure as he could in what pleased *us*.

I can't always recall to which of various childhood passions— ice hockey, sailing, and racquetball—he introduced me or in which ones he followed his wayward son. Some of them, though, must have flowed from me, and, when they didn't, his physical limitations dictated almost from the start that his desire our companionship played a large role in reviving limited skills. A one-eyed racquetball player is close to impossibility, but my father kept at it through years of dislocated shoulders and turned ankles because of his teenage son's aptitude for that sport.

We take in many things at empathetic moments when we recognize equally shared humanity, and amongst them are experiences upon which philosophy trades—the shared experience of struggling to say what we mean, the shared ability to reason about life while living it. We see another person with a story to tell who is trying to live as well as they can without fully understanding life. Elements of this experience can be deceptive and self-deceptive—for example, when people assume identities based upon prejudice or ignorance—but, whether the philosopher is actually perceiving the genuine humanity in the other, it *feels* that way. Besides a shared connection based upon empathy, the *ethic* of social connection, has something egalitarian about it: we're all in this business of figuring out our lives together! And that's the path that specifically philosophical dialogue sets us upon.

The continuity between schmoozing and philosophical dialogue is important. Perhaps this is why Socrates, that famous socializer and gadfly of Athens, persistently refused to lecture, give speeches, or write down any systematic exposition of his thought. Instead, he just hung out in the *agora*, the marketplace of Athens, having philosophical conversations.

As Plato witnessed, the philosophical commitment to dialogue goes even further than identifying an egalitarian interest in the other's humanity. For Socrates, what additionally leveled us all was our common fundamental ignorance. As Plato explains in *The Apology*, Socrates commits his life to demonstrating that "in fact the god alone is wise" and "human wisdom is worth little or nothing" (Apology, 23a). He does this by challenging various Athenians who harbor pretensions to "know" about life. He goes to the powerful groups of politicians, craftsmen, and poets and challenges each to prove its smug claims to wisdom. Each group fails to demonstrate any substantive wisdom and only ends up spitting mad at him for showing them up. All the knowledge we can build up about the world (by ourselves and without conversation) cannot tell us about our fundamental human condition. Given this, the only way to approach each other honestly is through dialogue and without making false claims to absolute wisdom.

Something else about Socrates' commitment to philosophical discussion is important. In the abstract, it sounds marvelously egalitarian, humane, and humble, but if Socrates himself is the exemplar, dialogue often seems, and perhaps really is, extremely arrogant. This relates to the historical context of *The Apology* itself, which recounts the trial and condemnation of Socrates in 399 BCE. Socrates' skepticism about human access to wisdom made him extremely unpopular with those Athenian statesmen, craftsmen, and poets who each *did* claim knowledge about life, but his skepticism also translated his own real humility *in his own case* ("I only know that I know nothing") into a social pose that could look like arrogance: "Whenever you claim to know what I don't know (about life, about the world)," he seemed to be saying, "*you* are more ignorant than me, who only claims complete ignorance." In *The Apology,* Plato holds the Athenians' annoyance with Socrates about thus claiming that *they* were more ignorant than him largely responsible for their decision to execute him.

My father followed Socrates partially: he could be whip-saw sharp in attacking what he saw as arrogant claims of unwarranted knowledge—taking on both fundamentalists' "proofs" for God's existence and scientists' counterproofs. However, he also embraced a concrete human "wisdom" that Plato's Socrates foreclosed—a conviction that experience taught us things through wonder about life and living that we could and did use in our everyday lives. Philosophical dialogue was my father's preferred *modus operandi.* In his hands this method trades both on what all people can feel certain about (the "meaning" of their own lives) and what they don't know (the meaning of life in general). It joins shared human experience with the enforced humility of those who are honestly ignorant.

The interesting question coming out of the trial of Socrates is how much of the tragedy between himself and the Athenians was just a "misunderstanding," something that another philosopher might avoid. If a philosopher, say my father, were more open and sympathetic in his relationships with his interlocutors, more able to hear where *they* were coming from, could he avoid the appearance of arrogance that condemned Socrates?

I think so. Lacking Socrates' need to defend his prophetic destiny (the declaration by the Oracle of Apollo that nobody knew more than him), my father was free merely to concentrate on the wisdom of the other person and to hear truth as they saw it. This allowed my father to polish a distinctly modern skillset: attention to the individual life of each and every "interviewee." My father saw the questions of how one should live and what makes one's own life feel meaningful as different and more subjective than those Socrates was asking. He didn't have to condemn *his* interlocutors for dishonesty or bad faith, as the Greek philosopher felt honor-bound to do.

This difference between him and his ancient predecessor sheds light on the tone of many of my father's dialogues in contrast to Plato's. Episodes of the "Paul Brockelman Show" were less like Socratic interrogations, more like what our joking title for his discussions suggest—a TV interview with philosophical questions aimed to call forth sympathetically the life views of the interviewee. In such situations, my father never felt obligated to expose people for fakes. For him, the fact that they had a life-vision—that they claimed in this sense to "know" something—*didn't* make them inauthentic. Instead, it meant that they had successfully navigated the shoals of "meaningfulness" and found a balance point, a way to quiet the knocking of anxiety at their door, and obtain some peace.

That is, my father would define the question of philosophical dialogue as an *emotional* one or, more precisely, the success of dialogue as a *matter* of feeling—what philosophers and psychologists call "affect." The philosopher has a *sense* of where the other person is coming from and, springing from that sensitivity, an emotional interest in hearing more from that person. In this view, the philosopher is much more like a good psychotherapist than a clever scientist. Common humanity provides the invitation to philosophy. This was the great *skill* that my father brought to philosophy and that I inherited, at least a little bit.

In praising my father as the great master of dialogue—like Socrates but without the obvious arrogance—I should also add that his greatest failures also lay in this realm. Each in our own way, my mother, my sister, and I all experienced moments when my father's openness turned out to be threadbare at best. Particularly as he aged, my father's commitment to such sensitivity ironically became what he most tediously lectured us about.

Between *myself* and my father, the tragedy seemed to be that he was much better at hearing voices from outside of philosophy than from within. My own choice to follow my father in career strangely removed me from the long conversation with him that had motivated my own career choice. I still remember both of our excitement when I approached him at sixteen and asked him to read philosophy with me. A bi-weekly "tutorial" with him ensued to discuss pages from Heidegger's *Being and Time*, but only briefly through one spring, enduring only in both of our memories.

Soon after my college years we arrived at that strange "agree to disagree" silence—surprising between two thinkers so close in every way—that ruled our relationship for the rest of his life. Perhaps beginning from my insecure need to build a philosophical persona independent from his, it certainly became mutual as my father aged and needed to defend his own identity against his narrowing horizons. Between us, what we most shared and brought us closer instead became a barrier, the semi-permanent fortification defining a long truce.

He never said so to me—how could he? —but I believe that this failure between us provided, alongside his fragile health, one of the great pains in his life. Seemingly, our relationship always remained strong, much stronger than his often- angry relationship with my sister. If things always remained polite between us, such manneredness indicated a mutual reserve, a prearranged set of "no-go" zones that protected both of us.

To his credit, my father never entirely accepted that unspoken truce. Instead, again and again, he would begin "the interview," clearly hoping to touch the wire that we both remember was so "live" that it determined my own career path. And yet, it didn't take but a minute for the probing to become something else. Like a nervous twitch, the "innocent" queries that helped his non-philosopher conversationalists to tell their own stories became direct challenges to me. For example, faced with my commitment to Judaism, in his later years he began to drop strange and pregnant hints about right-wing Israeli politics in my presence: "So what's to be done about those Jewish settlers on the West Bank, Tom? Aren't the rights of Palestinians important?" Clarifying my own decidedly Left views about Israeli politics and declaring support for Palestinian rights never placated him. Obsessively, his interventions always cast me, as a self-identifying Jew, into a rabid sabra fascist. I think a lot of this was just aging on my father's part, and I'd be mistaken to see real malice there. He often covered these odd outbursts with a grin and apparent curiosity: he was just looking to spark conversation! Don't be so defensive!

The human drama between my father and me always seemed to depend upon this paradox about philosophical dialogue: his famous openness was always circumscribed, limited only to *certain* kinds of response or discussion, certain life-attitudes. My life led me outside those boundaries and created never-resolved tensions between us; after college when I began to identify as a Jew, in my growing commitment to a certain "modern" vision based on Enlightenment values that he blamed for what was wrong with the world, and in an existentialist atheism that I began to explore after reading Freud and some of his followers. My long conversation with my father shipwrecked on those rocks and we never entirely escaped.

When it came to maintaining a genuine philosophical dialogue with his son, this foundering indicates an insight that is itself philosophical. The commitment to a life lived through dialogue must be *itself* like a dialogue—experimental, open to revising its specific beliefs, preliminary and catholic in its practices. Even the philosophical commitment to that openness that

63

my father traced back to mystery cannot stand on its own—it prospers only when one genuinely nurtures it in the way that Socrates prepared, the soil of conversation. When we forget that the truths to which we dedicate our lives must first and ever again be found in dialogue through shared discovery, we lose them. Too easily, all the best commitments—to truth, to love, to mystery even—transform over time into blood-sucking vampire-doubles, narcissistic obsessions instead of life-affirming opportunities to share. My father was right to demand that philosophy take place in dialogue, even if he sometimes sadly failed the test of his own imperative and his own great talent.

MEDITATION 5 THE USES OF PHILOSOPHY

What is philosophy for?

1.   In response to my childhood questions about what in the world my father *did*, what this strange "philosophy" thing was, I remember him telling me one of his favorite Søren Kierkegaard stories. He quotes it in his own book, *The Inside Story.* It's from the Danish philosopher's *Concluding Unscientific Postscript* and happens this way. The middle-aged Kierkegaard is sitting "in The Frederiksberg Garden, smoking his cigar and contemplating what he should do with his life."

> So I sat there and smoked my cigar until I fell into a reverie. Among others I recall these thoughts. You are getting on, I said to myself, and are becoming an old man without being anything, and without really taking on anything. Wherever you look about you on the other hand, in literature or in life, you see the names and figures of the celebrities, the prized and acclaimed making their appearances or being talked about, the many benefactors of the age who know how to do favours to mankind by making life more and more easy, some with railways, others with omnibuses and steamships, others with the telegraph, others through easily grasped surveys and brief reports on everything worth knowing, and finally the true benefactors of the age, who by virtue of thought make spiritual existence systematically easier and yet more and more important. And what are you doing? Here my soliloquy was interrupted, for my cigar was finished and a new one had to be lit. So I smoked again, and then suddenly this thought flashed through my mind:

You must do something, but since with your limited abilities it will be impossible to make anything easier than it has become, you must, with the same humanitarian enthusiasm as the others, take it upon yourself to make something more difficult.

My father always told this story with a grin, because it was both perplexing and deeply true. Typical students in introductory philosophy classes soon learn just how much a philosopher's work is to make things "more difficult," as their arguments are dissected for logical consistency, their assertions tested against experience, and the history of thought, their easy opinions shown to contradict one another, and so on. Soon they go from garrulous opinion to the lowering silence of wounded egos. Kierkegaard's vision of the philosopher reaches all the way back to ancient Greece, where, as we've already seen, Socrates inspired anger in those he challenged. Socrates left behind a trail of sufficiently bruised egos that a jury of the resentful condemned him to death.

But there's another way of understanding what Kierkegaard meant in *The Postscript.* The neat thing about that passage is how explicitly *modern* it is in thinking about the philosopher and society. Kierkegaard compared his own life to all of his friends who, in good modern fashion, were engaged in useful pursuits—business, medicine, even the Church. It's always been true that most people want to be useful. But our world tends to magnify usefulness and the pursuit of concrete goals through clear ends. While that emphasis is inevitable in a society that believes in human progress, it submerges other elements of human experience. So we must understand Kierkegaard's joke as a way of resisting our tendency to reduce *everything* to usefulness. He's playing with claiming his own idleness as a vocation.

The never-finally-answered question, "What is philosophy?" is part of philosophy itself and a key part. Because of this openness, philosophy *cannot* take the shape of a "useful science," and studying philosophy is different than any of the other knowledge pursuits. The necessity of determining, over and over again, just what the philosopher is doing will always block his or her rapid "progress." A secret of teaching introductory philosophy is the apparently sadistic pleasure—my father's grin, Søren Kierkegaard's self-satisfied cigar smoking—that all philosophy professors get at the moment when this begins to dawn on our students. In my own teaching, this is always a key pedagogical moment, when my good, pre-med, pre-business, or pre-law students realize *just why they hate this kind of stuff*! My father was a great teacher of philosophy and he could afford to get those practical folks all riled up about this useless course and later still bring them back to him with storytelling that put them right there, at the edge of their seats.

Maybe the way he looked also helped to draw them in. One day, somebody (I never learned if it was my father, my mother, or a friend) stuck a picture up on our kitchen bulletin board. It looked a bit strange but seemed like a photo of my father reading. In fact, it was Abraham Lincoln, taken in his last years. My mother laughed and tousled my father's hair: "you really are the spitting image, Abe-y Baby!" The name stuck in the family, with "Abey-baby" a household fixture for the next thirty years, long after my father had outlived Lincoln's 56 years and ceased so much to resemble the dead president.

Abe and Abe-y Baby: The Lincoln Resemblance!

By the time I appeared, my father had apparently settled into the quintessential philosopher's personality, the personality of the kindly but bumbling professor, to match this appearance. My sister and I both knew that we could best wheedle an extra quarter from him if we presented ourselves as denied some pleasure that other kids on the block enjoyed. In his later years such a soft spot led him to work for *Hospice,* providing companionship for the dying. Worry or pity could always move him to help. However, he combined this kindness with an abstraction that suited the classical philosophy professor. In his dialogue, *The Theaetetus*, Plato uses Thales to model this archetypal philosopher: distracted by the beauty of the heavens on a starry night, the ancient geometer and philosopher supposedly fell down a well – too taken up with "higher" matters, says Plato, to notice what lay at his feet

My father's kindly but slightly lost persona also had a more particular origin, a basic gestural hold on his being that certainly reached back *before* he became a professor. My mother always told the story of the time, while the two of them were living in Tübingen, Germany, when she developed a sudden fever. Always worried about her, he rushed her to the excellent university clinic there, insisting that she see a doctor, though it was Sunday. My mother spoke almost no German, so Dad took up the burden of communication. However, when the harried doctor entered the examining room, my father was so entirely absorbed in reading Nietzsche that he forgot more than the German language! The ensuing exchange—Doctor: "Guten Tag, ich heisse Dr. Schmidt." My father: "Ah, guten Tag, ich . . . bin . . . auch Schmidt"—went down in family lore. What better example of Plato's otherworldly philosopher could one find than Paul Brockelman, the man who forgot his own name!

Coupled with his narrative skill, my father's Lincoln-Thales schtick seemed to work on his students. They adored him, in ways that kept them sitting through the "useless" lessons to which he subjected them.

So, the philosopher makes life harder, stopping us in our busy tracks and even diverting us into different and more "philosophical" ways of living. If you think about it, such diversion takes us from blind following of social expectations to a protest against those expectations, or at least against their thoughtlessness. From the town square where society forms our desires and expectations—the Agora—the philosopher directs us into his study, his lair—a setting for the highly individual discovery of what lies beyond the useful. We must be alone again in the place of thought, of criticism. That was my father's point. That was Kierkegaard's point.

Despite the basis of his vocation in empathy and a certain sociality, that is the reason my father also imagined himself, as we often imagined *him*, alone. There, circa 1967, sits my father in his upstairs study at home, puffing on a pipe, and pouring over the latest from Jean-Paul Sartre, Hannah Arendt, or Paul Tillich. I later inherited his library, which consisted of hundreds of thoroughly defaced paperbacks, underlined, dog-eared, and thoroughly covered in his scrawling cursive annotations. So deep was his concentration on these texts that he often failed to notice when he knocked over the pipe and sparks fell into his overstuffed chair or onto the rug. I remember the stink when one chair began to smolder and the firemen rushed in, dragging it to the sidewalk below as the cloud of acrid smoke dissipated from the upstairs window. Even when his seven-year-old son insisted on playing at his feet, my father was a man alone when he worked in his study, a figure in the mold of Rembrandt's "Philosopher Reading."

But I don't think Kierkegaard is completely right in picturing the philosopher as a "useless" recluse. Ironically, I learned something else about philosophy from my father, the teacher, and another image of the philosopher. In my mind, he's wearing the blue jeans and open shirt that comprised the uniform of the day for the leftist academic, and he's introducing political comedian Dick Gregory to a crowd of adoring students. It's all very college-campus-in-the-sixties, very committed but also very irreverent and funny. My father has them laughing in the aisles with his Dick Nixon jokes even before Gregory steps to podium. I adore my father for his commitment. I always stand near the front, because I'm the official flower child of the student community. But more than that I stand in awe of my father's remarkable engagement with urgent issues of his day. As I look up at him, I think, this is what it means to be "a man among men." He knows what he stands for and he is unswaying in his *passion*.

It's true that much of that commitment remained a way of standing outside of society—of seeing the constrictions caused by the status quo without a clear idea of an alternative world. But there was something more, a positive vision that you could see in his confident bearing in front of any room.

One of my father's other *leitmotifs* was his discomfort with the reality of professional philosophy. This might seem surprising, since he had so obviously constructed in the classroom a philosophical world to which he was fully committed. But what I think this discomfort meant had to do with the purpose of academic philosophy as a teaching venture.

Our cliché about philosophers is that they are committed to rationality and science. There's some truth to that if we're describing the way philosophy is *generally* taught. In a standard American introduction to philosophy, the student learns a series of "positions," rational views of the world or of personhood that we associate with major historical figures and contrast with one another. If any course introducing philosophy, you'll likely run into this traditional way of studying particularly the Greeks. You'll learn, for instance, that Plato believed that "the forms" underlay all material reality and that no human being knowingly does wrong, while Aristotle challenged Plato on the nature of reality while agreeing about ethics. Philosophy emerges therefore as an historical series of "positions" that philosophers have held.

We might relate my father's discomfort with the enterprise of the academic philosopher more precisely to a recent development in the history of philosophy. French scholar Pierre Hadot has transformed the study of ancient "classical" philosophy (that from Greece and Rome) by challenging that common prejudice that we comprehend such philosophers exclusively through a series of contrasting views on controversial topics.

Hadot doesn't dispute our understanding of such positions but he does put them in a shared context: all of the important ancient Greek and Roman thinkers understood the common task of philosophy as re-forming people so that they would lead a recognizably "philosophical life." While the vision of such a life varied considerably, all versions of it were taught in "schools," institutions where people actually practiced living together "philosophically." Variations on this form of life involved anything from modest diet, celibacy, and wearing dull robes to public sex or mandatory participation in political life.

All of the positions of Plato, Aristotle, and the others actually fed into and were justifications of the various ways of living that their "schools" put into practice. For example, if the mind alone could access reality (Plato), then we should ignore the promptings of our passions. Even in advocating isolation and meditation for the philosopher, the "school" saw these practices as the necessary response to the weaknesses of human society. Philosophy was thus a life-choice *in society*, like joining a religious movement or becoming an artist. So its meaning was primarily social—preferring one way of living among people to others.

The flip side of his disdain for the "academic" version of philosophy, my father's vision was precisely a renewal of that ancient view of philosophy as some particular form of human life. My father wanted to lead and teach an admittedly new kind of "philosophical life," one that broke down the boundaries between philosophy and spirituality. Being his student was to change one's life, not simply to study and dispute positions about things! In some ways, this corresponded to an expectation that naïve students often bring to the classroom. Expecting to learn something like a "way" that one finds in many Asian philosophies, they get instead a disappointing series of views and doctrines. My father gave students something closer to what they were looking for. In my father's view, philosophy neither makes life easier nor harder. Rather, like a religion, it simply re-forms it, giving it a shape and direction. And in that sense, philosophy *is* useful.

2.　　　After college and marriage, my father went off to Evanston, Illinois, where he dove into philosophy at Northwestern University. At that time, Northwestern was famous for the study of "continental" philosophy, meaning philosophy that originated on the continent of Europe as opposed to England, home of what's still called "analytic" philosophy. Even when it admits its impossibility, the analytic tradition dreams of making philosophy into a science, fully compatible with the natural sciences that its philosophers so admire. The key difference for my father was that the continental tradition remained closer to arts and literature, so including in philosophy much more than a narrow emphasis on reason or argumentation. Really, my father was passionate about two philosophical movements coming from the universities and cafés of Europe: "phenomenology" and "existentialism."

Though more academic in its origins than its "existential" twin and more at home at the university and less at the café (or grocery store), "phenomenology" became my father's lifelong passion. This was precisely because it came from a rebellion *against* mere academic abstraction, even though it was a rebellion within the world of the university. What phenomenology "means" is a long-running dispute revolving often around the obscure texts of the German Edmund Husserl and a few other "founders," but on the whole the movement emphasized looking at experience *without* the lenses produced by social conventions, ideologies, and habits. As my father put it, the phenomenologist asks, "Stripping away all the expectations and cliches, how do we really experience a mailbox? Or sadness? Or dying?"

From the time of the movement's foundations by Edmund Husserl in the first years of the 20th-century, phenomenology stood for a return of philosophy from academic abstraction to what phenomenologists called the "lifeworld," the world of actual human experience. "To the things themselves" was Husserl's war cry that captured the spirit of a philosophy tired of endless academic abstractions.

Considerable debate about where precisely to search for such naked experience has ensued: how much does society or culture itself produce it, for example? Husserl apparently spent his entire life trying to clarify this and related questions, recording his search on an endless supply of café napkins and coasters bearing complex and cryptic notes to himself. However, my father's idea of and commitment to phenomenology were simple and stable: philosophy should come from and articulate some basic and shared life-experience rather than engaging in endlessly more refined abstract academic debates and distinctions. Moreover, his directive had a clear implication: because human beings experienced their own lives as and through narrative, phenomenology must concern such tales. As he concluded in *The Inside Story*, "Experience is best perceived through stories rather than abstract concepts." He went on, "If a person is asked what she has been doing or why she did it, she will normally give an account in terms of a story."

My father was a passionate phenomenologist precisely because he was a passionate storyteller. That was the great virtue of his teaching. For example, he peppered his account of medieval scholasticism with the story of the jealous search for Thomas Acquinas' body after his death—a search so desperate that finally his fellow Dominicans boiled him down, so they could better hide the remains of the substantial soon-to-be saint from pilgrims searching for a finger or other "Saint Thomas" keepsake.

My father needed the rapt attention of his audiences for it opened them up to *what* he had to say, to that difficult message of mystery that was always his primary text. Because it draws you in emotionally, your first response to a story is not skepticism or challenge but an effort to learn from it. Story telling was a defense mechanism, a way of establishing the right kind of response to his teaching. That was the real nature of his commitment to phenomenology, this otherwise obscure European philosophical movement.

The second pillar of my father's commitment to philosophy is harder to pigeonhole, although he spoke of it as "existential," referring to the movement called "existentialism," a still-persistent topic today on college campuses. My mother joked about how my father followed her around the supermarket with a copy of a favorite existentialist text, Nietzsche's *Thus Spoke Zarathustra*, occasionally reading a juicy passage amongst the broccoli or soup cans. This seemed fitting for the young man who was so bored in his father's grocery store.

Among the existentialists' various interests and understandings, one common focus was upon those experiences that defied systematic comprehension by reason. For Jean Paul Sartre and others, the distinction between "existence" (the simple fact *that* something is) and "essence" (what it is) underlies such moments where experience overthrows the capacity of the rational mind. Usually, the mind's effort to order and explain the world around it delineates our experiences: "That's a yellow rose, not a red one." "We're in New Hampshire, not Vermont." Every assertion about what something is winnows experience down from a finite set of possibilities. The experience of existence erupts against these rational limitations. Sartre's 1938 novel, *Nausea*, includes a diary entry of his fictional narrator, Anton Roquentin, that gives at least one account of such an eruption:

> So I was in the park just now. The roots of the chestnut tree were sunk in the ground just under my bench. I couldn't remember it was a root anymore. The words had vanished and with them the significance of things, their methods of use, and the feeble points of reference which men have traced on their surface. I was sitting, stooping forward, head bowed, alone in front of this black, knotty mass, entirely beastly, which frightened me. Then I had this vision. It left me breathless. Never, until these last few days, had I understood the meaning of "existence." I was like the others, like the ones walking along the seashore, all dressed in their spring finery. I said, like them, "The ocean is green; that white speck up there is a seagull," but I didn't feel that it existed or that the seagull was an "existing seagull"; usually existence hides itself. It is there, around us, in us, it is us, you can't say two words without mentioning it, but you can never touch it. When I believed I was thinking about it, I must believe that I was thinking nothing, my head was empty, or there was just one word in my head, the word "to be." Or else I was thinking . . . how can I explain it? I was thinking of belonging, I was telling myself that the sea belonged to the class of green objects, or that the green was a part of the quality of the sea. Even when I looked at things, I was miles from dreaming that they existed: they looked like scenery to me. I picked them up in my hands, they served me as tools; I foresaw their resistance. But that all happened on the surface. If anyone had asked me what existence was, I would have answered, in good faith, that it was nothing, simply an empty form which was added to external things without changing anything in their nature. And then all of a sudden, there it was, clear as day: existence had suddenly unveiled itself. It had lost the harmless look of an abstract category: it was the very paste of things, this root was kneaded into existence. Or rather the root, the park gates, the bench, the sparse grass, all that had vanished: the diversity of things, their individuality, were only an appearance, a veneer. This veneer had

melted, leaving soft, monstrous masses, all in disorder, naked, in a frightful, obscene nakedness.

Like Sartre, my father wasn't just committed to describing experience in general. The purpose of *his* kind of phenomenology was the description, above all, of the singular experience of "naked" existence. What Dad and others called "existential phenomenology" (an admitted monstrosity of word-salad but a beautiful idea!) was an effort to tell as a story what the person experiences when pulled away from the everyday tasks of analyzing, categorizing, and quantifying. Existential phenomenologists wanted to describe the experience of wonder, of mystery—what Sartre called "nausea."

The conceptual marriage of "existential phenomenology" was ideally suited to my father in the way that it joined the social engagement of storytelling with the ultimately isolated nakedness of "nauseous" existentialism, repeating that oscillation between Plato the scholar and Socrates the man of the marketplace that apparently haunted my father.

So my father conceived a heady ambition: he would teach a new kind of philosophical life, a life organized around the numinous experience that had transformed him. In this new teaching, academic study and the knowledge it generated really would amount to a "discipline," to a new way of paying attention to the heart of experience beating beneath the veneer that rationality provided in its efforts to control the world.

MEDITATION 6 EXISTENCE AND ETHICS

What makes a life worth living?

My father always hated the moral relativism that he saw sprouting up around him as he aged. Like many others, he labeled this "postmodern." Since ancient Greece, one of philosophy's basic suppositions has been that some lives are better—happier, more useful to humanity, wiser—than others. This doesn't mean that we should condemn any particular human being as unworthy of living. People may do their best and variously enrich the world while struggling with poverty, pain, disease, disabilities, and so on, even if they can't approach the life that the philosopher would point to as optimal. Allowing such variation doesn't call into question that the philosopher *does* hold one particular life to be better than others. As my father would say, all the wonderous variety in abilities and desires in persons doesn't challenge the fact that only those who work to strengthen certain basic human characteristics can reliably come close to fully realizing their potential.

One of the remarkable moments in S*eeing Life Whole Again* comes in its conclusion, where my father argues that the consciousness of wonder that he has described and praised throughout his manuscript and life's work should lead to an ethic of "mindfulness." He succinctly defines this ethic as "the attempt to bring that awareness of the mystery of existence into being and to live it by making it the meaningful *telos* or goal of our everyday living." A "mindful" person lives a life displaying awareness of the mystery underlying our existence.

Having proposed such an ethic, my father suggests that it is an "absolute truth" of human existence that we should realize this inherent capacity to live in the light of such existential mystery. The "good life" for those persons able to afford it, no matter where or when in history, will always involve some element of mindfulness.

Sometimes, we experience advocates of specific ways of life as arbitrary or even bossy and bullying, willing to impose their vision on others. Lest my father appear arbitrary or even authoritarian in demanding a certain kind of life from each of us, let me translate this vague language of "mindfulness" into another vocabulary that my father frequently used— namely, the "openness to growth through new experience."

We tend to lose sight of wonder because we only wear the "glasses" we acquire from anxiety, fear, the need for security. Those lenses transform experience into a problem we need to solve, reduce "what" we experience to beings or entities, and necessarily exclude "the mystery of being" (*that* things are at all). The major reason that we *fail* to be aware of the wonder of being—the awareness realized in mindfulness—is what my father calls a "fearful compulsion to control everything." So that wonder equates to what he calls "letting go" of that compulsion, a willingness to open up to life and our own potentials beyond our present identity. My father's ethical imperative is his demand that we crack open the hard shell that we form over time— what protects us from the world and shields us from our own potential as selves— shedding it so that we can grow.

It is not a call (never mind an imperative) that we live any particular "lifestyle." No mandatory prayer mats or yoga sessions! That is, the content of this ethic is open, like the basic ingredient of a liberal arts education—an education that is supposed to be transformative in exactly this way.

While my father's absolutist ethic is broad and liberal in its scope, with many kinds of lives fitting within it, the hard truth for him is that certain lives must count as "failed," bad, or just disappointing. This isn't to say that good can't come from those lives, but it does assert that such a life fails to reach its own potential, that something about it makes you shake your head and mutter, "What a shame!"

I am thinking of a particular life that had a profound influence on the formation of my father's philosophy   that was the life of his own brother. A psychotherapist amongst her many identities, my mother said that Uncle Henry was a classic Asperger's Syndrome case born too soon to receive the diagnosis. His was a sad life. He was the older brother whose age chained him to a career in the family business that my father avoided when he ran away to poetry and philosophy. While a clear path and concentration in engineering at MIT suited Henry, the grocery business certainly did not. He really just couldn't deal with people, their demands, their desire to be met where they were, their anger and suffering. As a result, the store that my grandfather gave him (the last of the "Brockelman's Markets" after Grandpa's early death), did badly and threatened to go belly up while Henry cowered in the back office toting up dismal sales figures. My father's intervention convinced Henry that he should hire a store manager and leave the people business to that person.

From then on, the store turned around, but Uncle Henry's life really didn't. He never married or even formed strong relationships beyond "buddies" from around his Boston suburb. My mother was not alone in speculating that maybe, in a fuller or later life, he would have been gay. But in the life he actually led, failure of connection was the outstanding characteristic. Even his few joys, above all owning and cruising a 26-foot sailboat, seemed to broadcast his need to wall out the world and create a small, controlled space for himself. I remember sailing with him and Paul on the *Ondine*, down below the Cape. A competent sailor, he was still consumed by a barely suppressed anger at the world. Sailing with Uncle Henry was always a brush with disasters narrowly escaped. He'd grab the tiller from me and bark orders in a hyperventilated nasal clip, his jaw set, amidst a long series of curses—as though care and attention to the sailor's world demanded an always simmering rage. That was the limit of Henry's emotional vocabulary.

Henry's incapacity to handle suffering and passion in any way other than furiously impotent protest against his own powerlessness was his undoing. In his early sixties Henry developed a case of vertigo that was relentless, driving him back systematically from all of his escapes. Sailing was the first to go.

He approached the problem rationally, had months and months of testing, all of it with negative results, until his doctors begged him to accept that the vertigo was largely psychosomatic—a grand trick his mind played with him. He refused to do this, moving directly from obsessive testing to a near-suicidal admission of defeat. Within two years he retreated to his small house and would only sally forth for his many doctors' appointments. Another two years found him in an assisted living facility and he was dead two years after that. In all that time, Henry fought his condition in the only way that he knew how—through desperate efforts to find a medical cause and cure for his ailments.

He never tried the alternative: to admit that he was sabotaging himself, that his inability to entertain passions, desires, and even experiences that he could not control must fail. That the world was bigger than the little box into which he tried to stuff it seemed to call forth a "disease" that took the vengeance of permanent loss of control on him. Every effort to "master" his disease pushed him further into helplessness and reduced the scope of his internal freedom. We all knew that Henry was condemning *himself* to death in the way most fitted for a fearful life.

In his last years, Uncle Henry was one of those angry old white men we hear so much about in the age of Trump—feeding rage off Rush Limbaugh and Fox News, addictively sending his money to one or another contest or get-rich-quick internet scheme ("you don't need gold bars; what you need is bargain soap chips!"), and hoarding the trash they sent him in his single room apartment in the senior living community. He died alone, and only his brother and I mourned him. It took us a week to clear a way through the unopened mail and chip bags in his living room.

My father and mother both died before I wanted them to. Both suffered from health problems that predictably shortened their lives—my mother's chronic smoking led to fatal lung cancer in her seventies. As I've already written, my father's youthful illnesses and accidents caught up with him at eighty. Still, my parents' lives were indisputably *full*. My mother was a professional dynamo—a path-breaking women's psychotherapist, and a painter of real note, much loved both by family and a large group of friends. My father's life was less unorthodox than hers but made every bit as much difference to the world. I mean "full life" here in the way we understand that term in our small talk: both had lives with full relationships, children, meaningful work. But I also want to speak of their lives as "full" in the more precise way that Dad means in idealizing the mindful life.

Take my father, in particular. Uncle Henry's life is worth recalling because so much of Dad's choice was clearly *not* to be his brother. Where Henry's emotional vocabulary was small and shrank to rage alone by life's end, my father committed himself to life-long growth and emotional openness. He followed my mother's lead in her exploration during the 1970s of group consciousness raising, and later my sister's various Eastern spiritual practices fascinated him. Even if he never immersed himself entirely in many of these "soul expanding" practices, he always remained sympathetic to them. He would never be a "brain over heart" guy like his brother.

That determination also underlay the strong, even violent choice that my parents' marriage represented early in their adult lives. My sister recently came upon my parents' love letters from their courtship. Those letters magnify the great and uncontrollable passion behind Dad's decision, against all reasonable expectations, to marry Barbara. Their letters also make clear that the strength of their common passion was a *necessity*, given the distance both had to travel to close the gap between their worlds. "My dearest Barbara," wrote my father, "my mother won't hear a word about you. She wants me to give up on the Romantic idol of marrying 'one of those people.'"

Both knew that they would face disapproving parents and disappointed suitors back home. The bond they were creating was a *difficult one:* passion gave them the courage they needed to remain open to each other.

When we speak of a "life worth living," the question arises from the perspective of the person living it. That's important to remember when considering what philosophers have to say about this topic. For example, in *The Apology* of Plato, Socrates famously comments, "For a man, the unreflected life is not worth living."

Students routinely imagine the Socrates who said this is a kind of Nazi who wants to euthanize all kinds of people—those living "hand to mouth" in poverty, those with mental disabilities, perhaps obsessive athletes—by condemning their lives as "not worth living." Even if we detect some arrogance in Socrates, the main point is that this famous pronouncement primarily refers back to the person making it—to Socrates himself. He is responding to the proposal from the court of Athens that *he* (Socrates) might save his own life if he just stopped philosophizing. His answer to that proposal is that, effectively, he would cease to be himself—to live a fully human life—if he allowed such limits on his thought.

He implies that others, too, should ask themselves what would happen to them if they agreed to a similar stipulation. This is different from demanding that every human being, whether able or not, engage in a life of philosophy. So, the question is always, "How should *I* live?" or "Am *I* living in the way that I feel—honestly, deeply—is worthwhile?" Socrates is demanding that *each of us* ask this question about our *own* life!

According to my father, these questions have teeth because there is a very real price to pay for failing to live "mindfully," open to the growth and the change that the world offers. To fail to live that way, to close the drawbridge, draw up the ladders and retreat into some inner keep, is really to cease living. I suspect that cases where the person seems to choose a kind of indirect suicide to shorten a life of despair and pain—like Uncle Henry—are more common than we like to think.

We all know of multiple instances where failure to grow has led to a kind of *metaphorical* death, to a zombified living death, where a person seems to be just taking up space. You show up for meals and collect your paycheck, but really are no longer there. It is not difficult to distinguish this from really living. Isn't such a living death the inevitable price of a deep failure of mindfulness?

In contrast, I attribute my father's many life comebacks to the remarkable way that he endured and continued to grow, not just through his encroaching deafness and blindness but also through my mother's many crises and even the grisly, dark months of her final illness. I remember his looking at me and asking, "Can things go on after this?" I remember his departure for Syracuse from his New England home of more than forty years. I remember his final two years there. Almost until the end, his was an examined life in which he always accepted a new adventure joyfully, if also with a quailing heart.

All of this returns me to the ethics of mindfulness. Perhaps what my father *doesn't* say about such an ethic is how much it makes the person vulnerable to circumstance. Ancient Roman politicians routinely committed suicide upon learning that their side had lost a dispute over senatorial or imperial power. Having publicly committed their lives to a cause, they had no "out" except the decision to die. I hope that "mindfulness" leaves more room than that for new possibilities to emerge unexpectedly in a life. Nevertheless, whether one is Henry or Paul, some moment seems to occur in every life when one faces checkmate, when a tired heart can no longer circulate enough blood to sustain thought, when nothing remains but an infinite fall. Even in a life as successful, as mindful, as full, as my father's, such eventual defeat remains. This inevitability of death is another of my father's themes and awaits another meditation.

MEDITATION 7 FRIENDS

How important is friendship?

There he is! Or, rather, there he isn't! That "he" is my father. In the University of New Hampshire student newspaper photograph from May 5th 1970, we most definitely miss him. Like the dog whole failed to bark in the Sherlock Holmes classic, my father's absence here was the key to a story. In the picture, his out-of-frame presence focuses the gaze of several hundred protesting students. The newspaper caption claims that he's addressing them. They're all looking at him, listening intently as he delivers advice. Actually, though I was only ten, I vaguely remember the occasion. With the help of some news-clippings, I can reconstruct both why my father was there and why he's not actually In the photo.

Paul Brockelman Addresses the Students of the University of New Hampshire May 5, 1970.

May 1970 was a most explosive moment in American history. My father threw himself into the fray, though slightly removed from the focus of attention. With news that Richard Nixon had sent American soldiers into Cambodia, college campuses across America boiled with anti-war protests and student strikes. In this context, a student's invitation to David Dellinger, Abbie Hoffman, and Jerry Rubin, three of the famed "Chicago Seven," to speak on May 5th at the University of New Hampshire seemed dangerous. Twenty four hours before the photograph was snapped, National Guard troops at Kent State University in Ohio had responded to campus unrest by firing on assembled students, killing four outright and injuring several others.

On the day of that photograph, both fear and anger were in the air. Nobody knew quite what would happen when the founders of the "Yippies" descended on the usually placid Durham, New Hampshire, campus. Following the complex negotiations that resulted in permission for the event, police and National Guard made their own preparations. In hopes of preventing violence, the University's president hunkered down with those troops at the Field House, site of the actual rally later that day.

My father was one of the few links between the groups of people yelling at and even planning harm to each other on that early May afternoon— "establishment" figures also sympathetic with the radicalized students. A popular young professor of philosophy whose lectures and seminars hosted the blossoming of political awareness and community, he agreed to become the faculty liaison for the UNH Students for a Democratic Society, the local branch of a national group that coordinated nationwide student resistance to the war in Southeast Asia. My father eventually paid a heavy price for his sympathy with those particular students. After the war, he faced ostracism. Nonetheless, his sympathy was never blind, and, for all the heady extremism of that moment, he didn't lose track of his own role as an older and wiser person.

That's what my father was doing at one o'clock on May 5th by the flagpole in front of Thompson Hall (T-Hall, everybody called it), the metaphorical center of the University of New Hampshire campus in Durham. He was exhorting the gathered riled-up to caution, arguing that what happened the previous day at Kent State could well happen in Durham, too. In the photograph, notice that none of the students have their fists in the air, despite this being a hilltop gathering for the purpose of announcing an outraged general strike. Rather, they listen quietly, soberly, as my father tries to take care of the community of young students whom he admittedly loved. One student who was there later wrote that my father's speech helped stave off what "could have been a disaster." He's calming them down!

The looming punishment for his alliance with the radicals is why the photographer has cropped my father out of the photograph. I remember overhearing this from conversations between my parents and their friends. The editors of the student paper, themselves some of the same radicals who organized the invitation of the "Chicago 3," wanted to protect my father. Everybody knew that he was there, that he stood at the center of the gathering in front of T-Hall.

So this photograph documenting a seemingly classic moment of historical anger and protest really represents friendship—the friendship of my father's students for him and his reciprocal friendship for them. Another contemporary photograph identifies many of those friends, the radical students from UNH classes of 1970-73. I remember many of them and two—Alice McKinnon and Linda Nestle (Allie and Ness, as my sister and I called them) —lived at some point in the extra room we rented out in our attic.

Both became family friends. Along with a supporting cast of other academics and artists, they were people we routinely welcomed to our dinner table throughout the late 1960s and early 1970s. I remember Alice in particular: while she lived with us, she was involved in an auto accident where a snowplow totaled her car. For months afterwards, she sat at our kitchen table and babysat my sister and me with a large cast encumbering her shattered left leg. Our favored activity at the time was drawing with a large box of Crayola crayons and Allie produced endless variations on a single image: a giant, yellow plow bearing down on a teeny VW, all of them captioned, "The Mother-F**ing Snowplow."

These were our friends, but especially my father's friends, who relied on and protected him on the 5th of May, 1970.

We owe to Aristotle the ideal of "philosophical friendship," of a friendship directed, above all, to the mutual recognition between friends of the qualities of humanity in each other. Under the heading of "friendship based upon virtue," the Greek philosopher poses a relationship that we can still idealize today, one where each friend wishes the deepest kind of benefit for the other—even, or especially, when such benefit doesn't obviously or immediately profit or give pleasure to the one conferring friendship. We might say that such friendship is humanitarian, rooted in something other than what Aristotle analyzes as "utility" and "pleasure," since it takes shape despite the lack of selfish reward for the person offering it. Thus, the friend "wish(es) good to . . . friends for their (own) sakes."

Such desired benefit is in part moral—we want the friend to become even more virtuous. However, Aristotle's idea of virtue derives from his central view that each being, and therefore each human being, has a specific potential or "good" to which they most deeply tend. Above all, the true friend wishes this good to her friend, but since such a realization of the other's potential will benefit everybody and not only the friend, Aristotle fairly underscores that "the good, in loving their friend, love their own good."

In other words, for Aristotle, the beloved good of the true friend is the shared potential of all good persons in the form it takes in a particular individual—precisely the friend's humanity. Always the acute psychologist, Aristotle calls attention to the dimension of friendship that allows us to overcome, to some extent, anyway, the petty jealousy we feel for others. He explains the joy that a friend feels when the other person "blossoms," comes into their own, becomes what they always promised to be.

Friendship based upon furthering that good in each individual will be far more stable than the infatuations that pleasure dictates or the relationships that occur when people make use of each other in business or politics. The purpose of the individual, the purpose of humanity doesn't change! Responding to the impatience of the young, Aristotle wisely insists that such genuine friendship takes time to develop.

I started by calling Aristotle's favored kind of friendship "philosophical," but we should not make the mistake of limiting that to philosophers. Aristotle also mentions the feelings of parents for their children and of soldiers for their comrades as related to true friendship. We see friendship's shadow wherever strong feelings lead people to wish for the deepest possible flourishing in others they care about. Still, those who are philosophers in that they are most skillful in pulling back from the web of pleasures and the desires they carry and imagining broader human good— those people *ought* to bring particular skill to friendship. Many of us do know what it is to genuinely care for someone. But we might consider the capacity for such friendship, and the realization of that capacity in one or two genuine friends, a key to fully realizing the philosopher's potential. If we take Aristotle's insight seriously, a friendless or even an "unfriendly" philosopher would be suspect.

This capacity for friendship most thoroughly set my father apart from actual other professional philosophers, many of whom I have observed can be wretchedly insensitive to people. Never was he without close friends. These included his comradeship with the painter Dirk Bach in the 1960s and 70s (he of the smoked banana-peel!). His alliances with those students at the University of New Hampshire included several who showed up more than forty years later at my father's memorial service. And his late "spiritual" friendship with Frank (See Meditation 11) was another that typified a life lived in deep friendship. This is all not to mention his more complicated relationship with my mother. Because he was interested in friends, and above all cared about them, people gravitated to my father, cared about him, wished him well, and, above all, loved him.

In those last two or three years after my mother's death, when the pain of losing her and the closing funnel of his sight and hearing drove him away from others, my father still formed *new* friendships as best he could. There was his passionate relationship with Louise (whom I'll discuss later), the woman with whom he fell in love at the end, and his eternally childlike intellectual enthusiasm joined him with like-minded others. He formed a connection with one or two members of the Jesuit community at my college in Syracuse, especially the distinguished astronomer, George Coyne, and he began to explore Saint Ignatius' *Spiritual Exercises*. As my father's health deteriorated, he gathered for lunches with George at Le Moyne College's Jesuit Residence, expressing the same excitement over intellectual possibility that I remembered from my conversations with him as a teenager. People flocked even to the ruin of my father like moths to a flame.

My father struggled mightily with his predilection for friends and companions. As a mystic, he wanted time alone, feeling that the experience on the shores of Lake Waushakum could only reverberate in solitary reflection. Mysticism demands the hermit's hut in the wilderness with piled-up years of solitude for ecstatic reading and reflection. My father's commitments to his friends didn't allow that, so he was always deeply torn between the reality of his connections to others and the dream of himself alone.

I suspect that he imagined for himself a gradual and gracefully increasing immersion in such hermit's mysticism as he aged. His own interests and his last texts—*Cosmology and Creation* and *Seeing Life Whole Again*—led him in that direction. The dilemma was that passion faded for him without friendship and *time* with friends. Retaining the philosopher's youthful mind required growing in friendship. Longing to be alone with his visions, he really needed to break intellectual bread with those around him.

My father's last decade with my mother was also the period of his retirement. One of their mutual friends was a successful painter who tried to help him with this search for meditative solitude, building him a small hut on the painter's wooded property up the Maine Coast. Warmed in winter by a small woodstove, my father could sit in the shack in a rocking chair and look out the single window at a beechwood. They made arrangements so that he could visit discreetly and not disturb the painter. But the hut never quite worked out. After half an hour at the shack, he'd be knocking on his friend's door, muttering something about the weather or their common interest in sailing, or even politics. Hours of conversation and dinner later, he headed home, a better friend but no deeper in his meditations. Eventually my father's failing vision limited even the twenty-minute drive to the cabin and visits tailed off. This became a sad monument to my father's vision of how he *should* live rather than how he could.

My parents' painter friend came to my father's memorial, remarking that his hut had stood empty a long time.

MEDITATION 8 GOD TALK

What do we mean by "God"?

When it comes to describing my father's teaching about God, his theological vision, I like the English-language expression, "too clever for himself by half." His was a brilliant philosophical idea and deeply true, but that cost my father dearly—first in the arrogance it provoked from him in the classroom and on the public stage, in how it sealed him off in the prime of his life from the discussions for which he hungered, and finally, in the mania or obsession it became as he grew old.

As a youth, my father learned the great trick of transforming vulnerability into the strength of openness and wonder, and here that hit its limit. Here, the one trick pony ceased to serve its master and ran away on its own. Don't misunderstand me: I don't think that my father was *wrong* about God. No, I remain utterly convinced of what he had to say about this. But this truth didn't set him free.

My father's story about God acted on him a little bit like the servant's behavior with Death in Somerset Maugham's re-telling of the tale from the Babylonian Talmud, *Appointment In Samarra*. Precisely his most strenuous efforts only led him into a fatal trap:

> There was a merchant in Bagdad who sent his servant to market to buy provisions and in a little while the servant came back, white and trembling, and said, Master, just now when I was in the marketplace I was jostled by a woman in the crowd and when I turned, I saw it was Death that jostled me. She looked at me and made a threatening

gesture, now, lend me your horse, and I will ride away from this city and avoid my fate. I will go to Samarra and there Death will not find me. The merchant lent him his horse, and the servant mounted it, and he dug his spurs in its flanks and as fast as the horse could gallop, he went. Then the merchant went down to the marketplace and he saw me standing in the crowd and he came to me and said, Why did you make a threating gesture to my servant when you saw him this morning? That was not a threatening gesture, I said, it was only a start of surprise. I was astonished to see him in Bagdad, for I had an appointment with him tonight in Samarra.

My father too tried and failed at the impossible.

When it came to God, my father made the case that most of us have no idea what we are talking about. My favorite Dad story here is that one night he came home and announced that some Mormons had visited his seminar on the Philosophy of Religion that day. Perhaps they came to expose Paul Brockelman, the dangerous heretic and atheist. We lived in the small state of New Hampshire with its McCarthyite newspaper, *The Manchester Union Leader*, which habitually "exposed" people like my father in its front- page editorials. The paper and its reactionary editor, William Loeb, had publicly called my father to task some months earlier, and he was no doubt benefiting from the fame that incident had given him.

My father was a classroom force, quite capable of turning the tables on thoughtless critics. Under that idiot grin he always carried into such situations, he would begin a friendly cross-examination of his foes. This was the conversation about God he had with the Mormons, who proved to be his perfect foils:

My father: So God is definitely a being?

Mormons: Yes.

My father: What kind of being?

Mormons: A man.

My father: What kind of man? How is he different from us?

Mormons: He's much more perfect and more powerful.

My father: Wait. if he's a man, he must have a . . . thing.

Mormons (used to this): Yes, of course. He is fully human.

My father: And this. . . thing, it, too must be more perfect and powerful, no doubt . . . bigger

Mormons: Yes.

(Laughter all around)

My father loved to school the religious literalism he detected in those Mormons. Its presence was a most sure-fire way to bring out a side of him that people wouldn't otherwise notice. His bearing *was* deceptive. During his "hippy" days as a radical professor in the late 1960s and early 1970s one might have mistaken him for one of his perpetually-stoned students, and he encouraged that impression, growing his hair (relatively) long and showing up to class in jeans and denim jacket. He even had his painter friend, Dirk paint one of his famed "postage stamp" images on the front door of our house, a sixties comic image proclaiming that this was the residence of "Dr. Paul, The Night-Tripper." All of this went quite well with his cultivation of the bearded "absent minded professor" look.

In fact, Paul only played the hippy, just as the musician, "Dr. John, The Night-Tripper" did too. But the image was convenient, partly because it obscured his razor-sharp mind so well behind a metaphorical cloud of smoke! Imagine the shock in exchanges like this one. My father hid a sometimes brilliant, even cruel Socratic ironist behind the professorial façade. Like Socrates, he was willing to pursue certain thoughts to their own absurd end and perfectly willing to crush a few egos along the way.

I mention my father's class with the Mormons because its irony points so well to the rather extreme idea about God that he embraced in counterpoint—which set the wheels of censure going in New Hampshire's newspaper in the first place. The good religious folk of New Hampshire were right to be offended by my father's heresy! The background to that idea appears repeatedly in his work, most prominently after the passage I've already quoted from *Cosmology and Creation*. There he expands on what we've already heard about his summer day by Lake Waushakum:

> My experience of wonder, that day, was at its core a noticing of reality itself, not this or that real thing, but the existence, the actuality, the is-ness I want to say, of everything. Wonder seems not so much an explanation or hypothesis about how or why things work as they do, but an experiential noticing or awareness of their being as opposed to non-being.

My father provided both a description and a philosophical frame for his experience: what comes forth in wonder is not any being (not any thing that could explain other things) but rather Being itself, reality itself—the reality of the real, the "Being of beings." For him, that was what people "really" meant when they spoke of God: God means what we experience when our entire experience is ripped open—Kaspar Hauser style—in moments of wonder.

"Damn the theology; full speed ahead to the wondrous!" That was my father's motto! You might say that his idea about God was "phenomenological" too. That is, instead of filling in our conception of the divine from qualities and characteristics we glean independent of our direct experience of "him"—say from the Bible or other religion—we learn directly from that experience, stripped to its bare bones. We experience overwhelming mystery and awe. *That* is God—not any being that "exhibits" those characteristics in addition to, say, creating the universe, performing miracles, or leading people here and there in old stories.

Despite the oddity of talking about God as the "Being of beings," my father's adoption of this understanding had a good philosophical history.[1] It's not difficult to argue that the most sophisticated theological

---

[1] It's important to note that this language of "Being" was another of my father's debts to Martin Heidegger. Heidegger's claim for the possibility that we might experience something that was not a thing ("no-thing," so to speak) struck many of Heidegger's contemporaries as absurd, and just this claim became a central hill on which the dramatic split of 20th-century Western thought into two very different kinds of enterprises was enacted. So-called "Analytic" philosophers followed Rudolf Carnap and the younger Ludwig Wittgenstein in a series of developments for which the "nonsense" of Heidegger's claim was exemplary of what any philosopher genuinely hoping to further human knowledge must avoid, while "Continental" philosophers (at first *on* the European Continent, in Germany and France, and then later in the US and around the world) defended or at least interpreted that claim. The fight over Heidegger became at least a proxy for a major split in professional academic philosophy.

versions of monotheistic religion historically asserted such an "identity" for God. My father loved to teach medieval philosophy with the main purpose being to demonstrate the centrality in medieval tradition of the idea that God includes Being itself. When he taught medieval, Augustine, Anselm, and Thomas Aquinas marched to his tune, and he argued that only with the modern turn of the seventeenth and eighteenth centuries and the onset of the "Age of Reason" did this mystical idea about God shrink in its philosophical prominence.

My father saw the mistake of those Mormons not *just* in making God into a man with a penis (they share this twist with all Christians). He saw the ground for *that* mistake in treating "God" as a "thing," a "being" at all. Of course, the abstraction of "reality," "being," or, God-forbid, "Being" (just what does that capital "B" mean?) indicates why historically we've all tended to fall back into an easier way of talking and the habit of treating God as a thing.

Particularly in Europe and the U.S., two important categories for the way we talk about "religion" put my father's lack of orthodoxy into relief. First, in everyday life don't we all agree that the defining characteristic of the religious versus the non-religious person is belief? Christians often refer to devotees as "believers." So right there in common language, we reduce the "what" of wonder or mystical experience to a being or thing, something that we might "believe in" or not.

That brings me to the second category that my father's polemics violated about God. Almost as old as the Christian emphasis on believing in God is the related assertion that *arguments* can bring us to firm and certain religious commitment. If your goal is the missionary's zeal, his sense of a contagious certainty about God, then nothing will serve you better than a set of such arguments. As with any thing, we can dedicate a science to proving or disproving it, and the results of that science will be particularly useful for those seeking converts.

Into the space that this assertion of logical certainty about religion creates steps the logician-professional philosopher, the expert in arguments, to offer proofs for the existence of God. For centuries, philosophers have trotted out such arguments or, equally, developed arguments *against* God's existence. Many have devoted entire scholarly careers to examining twists in logic that proofs demanded. Either way, philosophers participate in reducing God to thing-hood, to an arid matter that they might prove or disprove.

At the same time my father was battling religious fundamentalism in his classroom, he was waging war against this argumentative philosophy. For him, the key thing about treating "God" through wonder or mystery was the category mistake in taking mystery as something subject to proof *or* disproof. If religion killed God by creating the "God thing" of believers, philosophy continued the torture, crafting a sort of God Zombie, a living dead "God of the Philosophers."

In my father's battles about God there is a fundamental contradiction in his character. Beside the mystic, devoting his life to numinous existence, we find the intellectual warrior, donning his armor to battle all takers—both fundamentalist believers and rationalist philosophers. It didn't much matter that, with a little bit of pushing, pretty much anybody would offend my father's religious principles. Having myself taught introductory philosophy students now for more than twenty years, I can say that I have yet to meet one who recognizes their God in "the Being of beings," even when concretely explained, as my father would explain it, through mystical experience. He wasn't wrong. I'm deeply, fundamentally in agreement about the matter to which he committed his life. But here was a deeply spiritual man who spent most of his life fighting those who might have been most sympathetic with that spirituality and helped him to grow in it.

Such irony that a philosopher of concrete experience spent his days battling the plain and concrete religious *language* people actually used to shape their lives, today's language in which God *is* a "being" or an "object." My father appeared to his students as a prophet, eyes shining with a moral vision that completely defied the categories of their own upbringing. This often was a powerful way to teach. As every good philosophy professor knows, students *can* be led out of the desert and they often like the journey.

Still, most students just scratched their heads when my father first thundered on about "the Being of beings" and the "power of Being." There's a wonderful, telling moment in *Cosmology and Creation* apropos this reception. He clearly understood that what he really meant philosophically by God will meet resistance and that the clever reader will respond to his philosophical *hocus pocus* about God not being any "thing" at all with the simple question, "Yes, but does God exist?"

So, he asks the question himself. He then spends most of a chapter in an extended retreat. He finds multiple ways to explain how that's the *wrong* question and how we are mistaking the nature of God when we understand him through the lens of arguments for or against his existence.

Finally, starkly, toward the end of the chapter, he just admits it: "No. God does not exist."

For all his acumen about how and why religious questions are framed wrongly, my father knew that he couldn't just deny those questions their validity and importance to those who asked. He couldn't escape the world he lived in. But he could spend his career as a teacher and a scholar more or less doing what he did to those Mormons that day—showing them that they didn't know what they were talking about, despite their religious fervor. Most of us are like those Mormons—mistaken and asking the wrong questions to correct our errors.

But we can also fall into a different kind of error than the one leading us to literalism and orthodoxy. My father's "original sin" here was his tendency to paper over the experience he thought foundational for any religion *with the intellectual act of combatting such error.* That is, my father retreated from part of his own experience by becoming the rational, argument-clad philosopher crusader, thus ceasing to be the mystical hermit. It was as though the act of *winning* the argument about God's nature for mystics prevented him from living as one of them. He changed into the very rationalist whom he vanquished. His collision with the growing world of American fundamentalism was convenient. Added to his battles with philosophical colleagues, that clash kept my father plenty busy through the years, busy enough that he failed to recognize how his own spiritual growth had ground to a halt.

If my father carried on an impossible battle with the world at large, he certainly had one convert, albeit a reluctant and largely silent one—me! To this day, I panic when somebody asks me if I believe in God. The panic does not arise because I am confused in what I think or feel about the topic—though at times that might have been true, too—but because, as his son, I really don't know what that word "God" means! More precisely, my father's way of using the term was rigorous, in line with how historical philosophers and theologians developed its meaning—but wildly different from the way most people in our world use it much of the time. All my life, his voice has whispered in my ear that, nonetheless, on the whole he was *right.*

The primary victim of this slippage in meaning was my father. After all of his passion for the classroom, his family, and his books, he failed to *develop* the spirituality he was called to. We can trace some of that failure back to his maladies and to enforced self-enclosure of someone going deaf and blind. But not all of it. For one thing, at midlife and still possessing his faculties, my father only glided around the periphery of the Unitarian and Quaker religious communities with which he most identified. My sister, a genuine enthusiast for today's applied spirituality, recalls later attempting to guide my father into Buddhist and Yogic practice at West Coast temples and ashrams, to little avail. In life, my father always remained a spiritual tourist.

I suppose this was a case of "let the punishment fit the crime," karmic punishment for my father via enforced spiritual loneliness. Lifelong, he reaped the reward of clear vision and unbroken faith in his philosophical understanding. But he also paid the philosopher's price: the loss of religion's emotional power for constructing a community and a life. One way to put this is to notice that my father, despite all his appeals to humility, carried a subtle and indirect form of philosopher's arrogance. His claim to figuring out the question of God, no matter how theologically astute, made him exactly the same as his rationalist and fundamentalist opponents—the dogmatic know-it-all.

From his muttered responses when I asked him, the issue was similar perhaps to what interfered with my own flirtations with Judaism. There's something fatal to the effort to integrate within a faith community when you know that most practitioners hold views that you would have to reject as superstitious. You find yourself embarrassed both for yourself and for them, never quite fitting in, then withdrawing from the whole enterprise. As an aside, one does develop an odd appreciation for the tools of traditional superstition—fear of punishment in an eternal afterlife and hope of reward—in maintaining the docility of religious populations. By the tenth century, Moses Maimonides argued already that these might be wrong reasons for engaging in religious practice. But in a complex world, there's nothing like fear to concentrate one's devotions. My father's alienation from communities of believers is an example of the inner dynamic that has alienated Western intellectuals from religious life since the Enlightenment. That dynamic remains a more potent force than even my father's philosophy could overcome.

MEDITATION 9 FATHER AND SON

Does all language tend to silence?

When I turned fifteen, my father gave me a sailboat. This *was* a noble gift, heartfelt and aimed to please me right down to my toes. Actually, the boat was quite modest—not at all a yacht or anything like that, but a twenty-foot Alberg Typhoon, a classic if slow design with a small keel and a minute cabin. In the years following, my father and I expended inordinate and unsuccessful efforts on constructing a platform that would allow this tiny space to serve for sleeping. Nor did Dad really give *me* alone title to the *Perelandra*. I shared ownership of this small vessel with a painter friend of the family and with my father too. But the gift of the boat was real. He would not have bought it at all except for me and it answered an ache in me that he knew better than anybody in the world.

For as long as I can remember, at least since I was seven or eight, a "Dad and Tom Saturday" consisted of an expedition "up the coast" after a hearty pancake breakfast to busy ourselves with sailboats. Not that we generally did any sailing, though occasionally we would volunteer to crew a friend's boat for a race or to cruise just offshore to the Isles of Shoals with my Uncle Henry. But we did *concern ourselves with boats*, visiting harbors and yacht clubs from Hampton Beach all the way up to Portland to see what was there. Perpetual sailboat tourists, we appraised the boats (depending on the season) sitting at slips or moorings or laid up and covered in canvas in the yard. I generally fell for a kind of racing boat, constructed in the 1930s or 40s from maple or even teak planks and varnished to a shining magnificence. My father knew the nightmare of entire winters spent in the frigid boatyard with oil and varnish, so he preferred boats that we might actually entertain owning. There was an episode in his later life when he and a handy friend actually went all-in on a 53-foot monster yacht built from cement, which stood for seven years in the backyard, demanding infinite repair. When I was a kid, we justified our ogling of sailboats by claiming that—one of these days—we were buying our own boat. But mostly, we took our day trips for the enjoyment of the coast, its greyish light and its damp wind, and each other.

My father's gift to me of *The Perelandra* filled that unconscious void in my teenage experience, intervening at that dangerous moment in a young person's life when he faces the possibility that dreams might remain entirely severed from hopes and so, as a result, will fail to believe himself worthy of *projects*. The trim boat with beautiful lines bobbed at its mooring in Kittery Harbor, a bike ride away from Portsmouth, and its care and feeding as well as sailing kept me busy over summers during high school. I constructed that unlikely and cumbersome sleeping platform and I tried using it one calm night, but the strong smell of gasoline below-deck ensured I wouldn't repeat that experiment. I also learned to jury rig the ancient outboard that supplemented the sails and, when such improvisation inevitably failed, could guide the boat to the dock on the power of our aged jib alone. And I sailed her, too—up the river or out of the harbor, never too far alone, but far enough for a sense of adventure accomplished. She wasn't everything I always wanted. She was what I needed then.

Because he gave me what a father *can* give who sees his son's needs far beyond my own limited understanding of them, I loved him with an all-conquering passion. I started my adult life as close to him as could be. That intimacy also explains how, in the following year when I was sixteen, he set me on the path to philosophy—explains that decisive tutorial, where I visited his smoky office every other Tuesday afternoon over a very long summer, to discuss the books of the existentialists. I argued with him even then, but mostly I just accepted instruction from him: "This is what Heidegger means by "being with." "Sartre's 'nausea' is really just another name for wonder, a name that betrays his residual French rationalism." The lessons were myriad, but mostly I just remember "getting it" —understanding for the first time what my father had given his life to.

Yet I didn't exactly take my father's path as my own. Pursuing academic philosophy of any kind seemed a cop-out for me, betraying a singular lack of imagination. Sigmund Freud described the need of sons to metaphorically murder their fathers, and I was no exception. The more my father's existential rightness moved me, the more pressingly I needed to find my own voice. That need, as much as the afterimage of those Tuesday afternoon sessions with my father, haunted my next ten years and my emergence into adulthood.

Because I loved my father so deeply, this "murder" I had to commit could only take a strange, convoluted form, like those movie smotherings of the inconvenient elderly relative whose presence crimped the protagonist's plan for escape to a better life. Violence mixed with affection and intimacy in equal doses. So, over and over in my young adult life I flitted around the flame of philosophy (*my father's* flame) at the same time I insisted on one conscious difference: this must be *my* life, *my* philosophy—not his.

If my young adult "mission" produced strange ambivalence in my behavior toward my father, his response seemed equally split. On one hand, I could see in the way he looked at me his understanding that I needed to act out, to play something other than the loyal disciple. I remember his acknowledging my independence then and later, too. Like a good Aristotelian friend, my father wanted his son to be himself, even if that meant embracing some things that he rejected. "You do what's good for *you*, Tom," he said. And he meant it.

On the other hand, I clearly possessed the weapon of all sons through history back to Oedipus himself: I could get under the old man's skin. What is the father's weakness? Where does his wisdom end? Leave exposing that to the son.

My own spiritual odyssey with Jewish religious experience deserves telling in relation to my ability to visit the tortures of Oedipus on my father. His reaction to me on this path was not the most flattering moment in his experience, but it does indicate something about where his philosophy blinkered him and what drove us apart in later years.

So what was it that so bothered my father? I think back to a moment and a particular Maariv, the Jewish evening prayer in Jerusalem. It's November, 1984, and I'm in the *beit midrash*, the "house of learning" of a small religious school on the city's outskirts. I have just returned from a lecture in the old city. Having intended my visit to Israel as a mere sightseeing expedition, I have ended up at this school for secular Jews, whose purpose is to bring them back to the traditional faith. While I remain skeptical of that overall project, I do find something powerful in the air. The walk I've just taken, the evening cool, a particular hush there that emerged with the night, remains with me as the prayer moves through its fixed structure to its center, the Sh'ma—the invocation of God's unity.

Something about the particular way that religious Jews pray that passage, the Sh'ma, in Israel—in my experience since, almost nowhere else—is unspeakably moving. Jewish liturgy oscillates between individual pacing and moments of unity timed to the voice of the *hazan*, the leader of prayer. The rhythm is one of individual initiative, almost anarchy, occasionally coalescing into momentary unity. The practice in Israel with the Sh'ma accentuates this rhythm, turning it into a wild and frightening creature with a life of its own. The difference lies in a preference, even in unity, for aesthetic discord over harmony. By contrast, many American synagogues actually unite in a melodic line for the words, *"Sh'ma Yisra'eil Adonai Eloheinu Adonai echad"* ("Hear, Israel, the Lord is God, the Lord is One. ...") with an effect that is, well, choral—all the voices intentionally harmonizing.

In Israel, the prayer embraces the greatest possible discord in unity. Perhaps part of this stems from the confident Hebrew of the Israeli orthodox, who loudly assert their own invocations wherever precisely they are in liturgy. Everybody seems to *howl* the key words together but in a voice anything but harmonious. Thus, even the moment of punctuated "unity," when the entire group asserts God's oneness together, comes through as maximally chaotic. That November evening in Jerusalem, the voices produce a remarkable cacophony that is nonetheless strangely united, unified in a manner beyond human comprehension.

Above all, juxtapose *this* unearthly "noise" with the hush of Jerusalem's early winter evening. This combination transformed my early adult life. For somebody who enjoyed the best literary education that his world could afford and who responded to it with years of intensive seminars involving reading in the philosophical and literary traditions of Europe and the United States I was, nonetheless, oddly distracted at that age. As a young man of twenty-four, I was largely unable to lose myself in the words and arguments of the many books over which I passed my eyes, somehow disengaged from the very world I dedicated myself to in my conscious life.

I'm sure that such distraction is common amongst the scholarly. For one thing, the life of thought and study that we idealize within the history of Western literary culture is unnatural for young human beings. Everything from the need for bodily movement to longing for love and sex strongly calls them. It's no coincidence that we conceive the scholarly ideal as monastic, ascetic, a denial of the senses.

But, in my case, all that common discomfort was focused through the lens of my father's thought. For him, combining Heidegger and Christian mysticism, the point of all that quiet study was less the rhythm of words and thoughts than the quiet itself. The goal of study and meditation was stillness. In this view, we must reject the chatter of everyday life in favor of silence or, even better, in favor of a kind of poetry that reveals the emptiness of such mere noise.

For the early part of my adult life, coming to terms with my own spiritual and philosophical commitments had left me both convinced of and strangely uncomfortable with this view. It's even arguable that I attended Yale as an undergraduate because of the way that it informed my first experiences of it during a summer visit in high school with my father. This conception fit into a vision of myself living a monk-like life of claustral discipline, observing a "rule" of silence as I studied the nature of Being. Yale's many collegiate gothic courtyards, enclosed cloisters, gardens, and bubbling fountains made a vivid impression on me. The inaccessibility of this student-monk's life oddly strengthened my fantasy: in summer many of the courtyards are only visible through locked iron gates. While actual student life at Yale, thank goodness, is far from satisfying such a monastic yearning, that glimpse of hidden gardens fed my fantasy too. The Yale of my dreams remained essentially mysterious, a reality always veiled and awaiting further discovery.

If you think of the ample *noise* I've described in the middle of Jewish prayer, perhaps the experiential ground of an ancient debate between Jews and Christians will begin to come into view. The powerful noise of discord only hints at a deeper difference between dominant Jewish and Christian practices. This stems from the disagreements out of which Christianity emerged and these define two thousand years of miscommunication and even persecution between these religions.

Begin from a more pedestrian distinction. The ideal of a religious life within the Christian world returns us to that vision of the monastic life, a fantasy reinforced by the extensive and even dominant history of such a life within Christianity since the fifth century "Rule" of Benedict of Nursia established this form of communal devotion and life within the European context.

If there's a parallel within Judaism to the monastery, a dominant Christian life form that combines religious devotion with a form of community, then really that form is the "yeshiva," or religious school. Beyond containing regular, periodically-mandated prayer, the practices of such a school are similarly religious in intent, but the spirit of the institution is quite different from a monastery. Traditionally, at a yeshiva, young men work in pairs under the guidance of older teachers (literally, "rabbis") to "learn" pages of the Talmud. These are the detailed texts and notations the Jews in Jerusalem and ancient Babel (Iraq) made about that part of "the law" ("Torah") not included in the written Bible. This unwritten law is even called the "Oral Torah" because it is a compendium of those parts of Jewish tradition originally handed down orally—also, I like to think, because it is something like a script for an ongoing oral practice. This odd religious ritual occurs in the dialogue between study partners, "*khevruta.*" Depending on its relative antiquity, each page of the Talmud contains a central section of text in Hebrew or Aramaic, surrounded by later rabbinic commentaries, written in a famously abbreviated, note-like fashion. Thus, a famous tractate begins with the Aramaic equivalent of "two holding a tallis" (a religious prayer shawl). The authoritative commentators included in the margins will have offered equally telegraphic commentary about these few words.

The task of the pairs studying the Talmud is to make sense of all the layers of text and commentary while bearing in mind certain basic interpretative rules. For example, as part of the Torah itself, at least the central text must be construed to be true—one cannot simply dismiss the central text as badly argued or even historically error-ridden. Furthermore, every mark within the text must have a function, since God doesn't waste words. And so on.

The religious imperative to obey those rules leads to oddly literal interpretation in which any interpreter must account for every word. As you can imagine, there are an endless number of ways to do that. That's particularly so when you add in the authority that many *previous* interpretations carry, which any new reading must also creatively take into account. The result of all of this is that the practice of this interpretation is actually one of equally endless dispute.

Some of the disputation arises because following the rules of interpretation often leads one to readings that directly *oppose* what the obvious meaning of the text seems to a casual reader. In one example, when the text says, "Moses went alone," it really means "with the children of Israel"! Most commonly, the arguments come from the apparent nonsense of an original text that one is still duty-bound to make sense of. How could Jacob walk from Jerusalem to Beth El "on his fingers," as the metaphorical Hebrew suggests?

The *activity* of the learning at such a Jewish religious school involves constant chatter or, better, ongoing constant argument. This is all conducted in a rising and falling singsong that, for thousands of years, Jews have found useful to mark the cadence of logic. Multiply that hubbub by the multitudes of pairs learning various pages of Talmud throughout a single *beit midrash* and you begin to suspect the life-basis for Judaism's peculiar relationship to language.

Into the pot I'd throw what I might call the "materialistic" prejudice of Judaism. All of those disputes are, in some way, *about* things—the prayer shawl ripped in half amidst a dispute about its ownership, the "Get" or writ of divorce that is valid or not depending on whom it strikes when thrown in anger, the ritual vessels that one may or may not use inside the precincts of the temple. In every case, the life of the yeshiva, the life of spiritual devotion, demands that we tarry with such everyday objects and, above all, with the words that invoke them.

We could not be further from the silence that Benedict's rule established and that the spirit of Christianity underscored even in Heidegger's existentialism. Further, as literary theorist Susan Handelman argued in her 1983 book, *The Slayers of Moses*, this tension is hardly accidental and highlights a deep cultural tension between Greek and Hebraic roots of Western tradition, Athens, and Jerusalem. For Greek philosophers from Plato onwards, the *"idea"* is what contains reality—the ideal form of the thing, beyond language and only inadequately indicated, in any given case, by words.

Handelman argues that historical traditions intertwine so that the attitude of Plato and Socrates helps create the view of silence in Christianity, which conceives truth as lying beyond the chatter of words. Here, Paul of Tarsus, a converted Jew, articulated the clear ethical ideal with his emphasis on "the spirit" over "the letter" in Christianity. As Handelman puts it, "The pure thought of ideas is silent, a dialogue of the soul with itself independent of language."

We can imagine the Greek philosopher studying the world as a spectator, somebody gazing at the idea as an image "in heaven" from which the world is copied. The Rabbinic tradition in Judaism demands that we think instead of somebody *listening* to words, and speaking them.

In the famous passage from the medieval Jewish mystical text, *The Zohar*, God creates the world from the letters of the Torah, providing perhaps the most striking explanation of the role of language in some equivalent to what we call "cosmology." Handelman explains that for the Rabbis, "The Hebrew word was not just an arbitrary designation, but an aspect of the continuous divine creative force itself. . . Names are not conventional, but intrinsically connected to their referents." In Jewish tradition, the name *is* reality, not an alienated image of it. This means that human usage of language—our speaking, and arguing and interpreting—is itself an extension of creation.

To put Handelman's thesis in a nutshell, Jewish tradition sees the world as *process,* as an ongoing event which includes human, historical interpretation, and exposition as part of itself, a continuous creation. Far from a simple knower attempting to frame true propositions about an extra-linguistic reality, the rabbinic interpreter is part *of* the action. His interpretive activity belongs to the significance of Being. In Judaism as an ethic, what we get historically is not a drive toward reverent silence but an imperative to ongoing disputation. Piety and humility mean entering the right conversation in the right way rather than silencing conversation altogether.

In November, 1984, this kind of sophisticated philosophical-theological speculation from Handelman and others didn't immediately occur to me. I remember from that fall in Jerusalem a sense both of contradiction and possibility much more immediate, much more powerful than that. Precisely the skills in listening to experience that I learned from my father told me that I had something important to learn from that moment, something that took me in a very different direction than the one that had pulled me along to that point. I stayed in Jerusalem for the year and later returned to the States armed with a vague commitment to Judaism and a strong impulse to the enthusiastic, devotional interpretative practice that I learned in yeshiva. Something about those practices of Jewish religious education energized me, ironically, to return to Philosophy, to apply to graduate school, and to undertake the labor of training to become a professional philosopher. I didn't know exactly what I believed. I certainly resisted the demands of the Jerusalem faithful who advised me to adapt the life of Jewish orthodoxy. Yet using the energy generated by Jewish affirmation of the world and its interpretation made clear sense to me at the most basic, existential level.

Often, clarity in one's life doesn't manifest as articulated belief or doctrine. After 1984, what allowed me to go on and grow was breaking with the fantasy of monastic silence and wonder that I had carried as a form of alliance with my father. At least, I began to suspect that the life I previously assumed as ideal wasn't right for me, that my own spiritual path might be more of the yeshiva student and less of the monk than I ever imagined. The complexity here was that my father could never really acknowledge this turn in my path. He certainly accepted my return to graduate study in philosophy and supported my applications to programs with colleagues of his from graduate school or conference life. But he resisted both my Judaism and what he took to be its intellectual offspring, a new kind of philosophy coming out of France called "post-structuralism."

I realize now that my father carried from his family an unconscious and therefore unquestioned antisemitism, even though he had already pushed it aside once before to marry my mother. I remember my non-Jewish grandmother's reaction when I returned from that year in Israel with my improbable heavy rabbinic beard and yarmulke, identifying as a Jew. She dispensed with my new identity in one sentence: "You're not Jewish." And that was that!

Dad was certainly more sensitive than Grandma Brockelman, but he never seemed able to enter into the dialogue with me that I hoped for about my Judaism and the sense of discovery I brought home from Israel. Mostly, there was that odd nervous twitch about Israeli politics and not much sense of curiosity beyond that. As I read and reflected more about the history of the Jewish/Christian standoff, this lack of curiosity made some sense to me. I had chosen to invest myself in a tradition that ill-suited my father's conceptual apparatus, something that his intellectual heroes had long ago rejected.

And so, less than ten years after the tutorials in Heidegger and other existentialists that had brought me to his feet, I left my father's discipleship. Actually, I eventually ended up not so far from him in my own intellectual life.

No doubt, my sympathy for Judaism and for the viewpoints of technology and science led me to listen more seriously to philosophers who borrowed from those traditions, and particularly to the "poststructuralist" French philosophers whom my father abhorred. But because I held onto my father's fundamental commitment to a universally recognizable human experience—a commitment rooted in moments like his description of what he felt standing by Lake Waushakum as a teenager—I also eventually found the abstract and convoluted intellectuality of Derrida and the whole post-structuralist French crowd unsatisfying. My father never acknowledged this proximity between us about either philosophy or about religion, withdrawing instead. He stopped seeking serious conversation with me, never really venturing to the curiosity about his own son that he gave to his students or even the plumber!

I won't claim innocence in creating the long truce between us that followed. We determined together the lack of growth in our relationship over the following years. But my father did seem to fail the test that his own son's development set for him. He never transferred the curiosity and wonder so present elsewhere in his life for my path. Surely Freud's Oedipus suggests that such failure is inevitable, that there must be something like this kind of tension between even the closest fathers and sons. I don't blame my father or myself for that long truce—but now I do regret it. I wonder what he and I might have built from the promise of my early years!

MEDITATION 10 MODERN TIMES

What is modern technology?

We who live today in a cloud of dystopian anticipation, of Mad Max deserts and Blade Runner cities, all those who are basted in continuous technological anxiety, will have little trouble in understanding why, at the end of his life, my father shared the mood of such fictions. As he grew old and tired, the curmudgeonly temptation to see a world "gone to hell in a handbasket" grew just too strong to resist. Or perhaps the substantial energy necessary to maintain optimism failed my father. The technological pessimism of my father's last twenty-five years seems more excusable in him than in the much younger scholars who suffer from it today.

Though an early blooming plant in his intellectual life, my father's own version of techno-pessimism only choked out a competing story about modernity, science, and technology in his last years. The other, the great story of modern times and progress held a powerful, always paradoxical sway in my father's life and sometimes in his thinking too. This *other* story was the very air that we all breathed as I grew up in the 1960s and 70s. In that world of constant technological, social, and political changes, the important thing was to value them and to shape them rather than becoming their victim.

This modernist view of life exemplifies the ethics that first shaped the 18th-century European Enlightenment. As philosopher Immanuel Kant liked to put it, people would embrace their own maturity, embrace the truth that nobody else (God, ancestors, traditions) could make key decisions for them. Historically, to embrace modernity is to affirm that no authority, no omniscient source of truth, guarantees the lives we choose to live. In this, the spirit of the Enlightenment belongs right beside my father's condemnation of superstition. At its heart, an emphasis on human autonomy is inseparable from a certain kind of optimism, a belief in the world as human beings have made it—though imperfect, containing possibilities for human happiness and growth. We can remake our own world after all, shaping it to our needs and desires. Progress is possible.

Both of my parents lived a life imbued with this progressive modernism. My father's own choice to teach philosophy seemed perfectly in line with the kind of optimistic vision that Americans prefer. This moral commitment shaped the way he approached his profession. Philosophy *could* be taken out of the ivory tower and returned to the concrete concerns of citizens, *could be* shaped to aid in building richer, more considered lives for a rising middle-class. In an odd way, his life project was part of the "American Dream."

That was also where the "Great Seacoast Salon" came from—the sense that my father and mother together were part of a broader project of social progress and, yes, liberation. I have a photo of my father and mother from 1972 in front of me—Mom with a large, Angela Davis-style afro and Dad with an unbuttoned polo shirt—that testifies to how this moment remade the two of them, at least superficially. But it goes deeper than that. Behind all the marches and late-night political meetings and the anger of those years, I think there was a peculiar optimism afoot in the cities and on the university campuses of America, the places that my parents called home. There was a sense that the world could be made better and that the crazy social norms they had grown up with could be recast. You didn't have to accept the marriage that your Jewish mother chose or the career that your Protestant father had prepared for you. Such optimism went through the wringer sometimes—think of the 1972 presidential race and the exposure of naïvete that led people like my parents to believe that George McGovern could win a national election. But even those crushing defeats seemed to leave open some path to social progress, some direction for the work that their lives underwrote.

After I grew up and left for college, my father's own lived commitment to that progressivism increasingly collided with a predominant *intellectual* story from his work, Martin Heidegger's account of the modern world. As became increasingly clear when *I* was in college studying philosophy, Heidegger's seminal thought evolved into an overarching

130

Barbara and Paul in Yugoslavia: 1972

criticism of the values of modernity. Though a bit extreme, in this it was typical of 20th-century philosophy from the European continent. Even as the Germany of the 1930s teetered in widespread instability during the Weimar years while Hitler and the Nazis rose to power, Heidegger developed a philosophical insight that tied the rise of modern science and the accompanying transformation of basic life conditions to what he called "the forgetfulness of Being."

For Heidegger, there was a clear bond between Western society's pursuit of scientific, economic, and social progress, and a utilitarian and practical ethic that hid what *really mattered* in human experience—what my father called "wonder." Modernity and modernization alike led to loss of meaning. Multiplying by a million times my father's personal rejection of the grocery business in Worcester, Massachusetts, Heidegger rejected the very successes of modern societies, especially how they diverted human energy into robotic "productivity" at the cost of genuine significance.

The very tools that the modern world projected (and still projects today) for bettering the human lot on a mass scale guaranteed a spiritual impoverishment of the human condition. They did this because they reinforced the human desire for *control* above all else. Within the modern context, when we accept a scientific result, that just means that we accept that anyone following precise experimental steps could repeat the result too, that some corner of nature (or human nature) is therefore "under control." We accept that a sheep can be cloned, or fusion produced without heat, when other scientists can repeat that result at will by using the same methods.

Over time, the blinding success of scientific method and its emphasis upon verification and repeatability reinforce those cultural areas where such progress is possible and direct and deemphasize those elements of culture not amenable to such modeling. We begin to lose even the language for developing understanding of that vague and all-encompassing realm that Heidegger and my father, following him, called "Being." "Forget all that soupy and vague stuff," implies the language of science! "Let's give our energy, our time, our professional lives, to areas where we can 'make a difference,' where we can extend control." Such powerful tools for both seeing the world and blinding us to how we create it with a billion daily choices are the glasses provided by modern science and technology!

That was certainly the way that my father used Heidegger's lens in *Seeing Life Whole Again* to diagnose the spiritual ailments of his own world. Even the Western spiritual/religious search for certainty (about God's existence, about one's own future) was essentially "technological" in this sense. And just so did my father see it. It came out of this quest for ever more control and security, rather than from openness to mystery. In an email exchange with a friend quoted in that manuscript, my father explains that the real spiritual challenge "was how to trust reality, plain and simple, not how to convince myself of the truth of some particular religious story or other."

My father converts Heidegger's story about science and control into a narrative about spiritual danger, in this way following through on Heidegger's suspicion of modernity. So modern progress is necessarily tragic, even non-existent. Every step forward in our ability to control nature (or God) accompanies a step backward in our spiritual being, as we reinforce our control over nature at the expense of our ability to experience wonder, to let being be. Progress is impossible, or, at the very least, incoherent.

Particularly through his later years, my father's Heideggerian pessimism about modernity gave birth to a twin phenomenon, an oddly messianic view of history that detected a transformative "post-modernity" as either right around the historical corner or already upon us. He anxiously awaited a kind of spiritual "new deal" when science and the mania for control would recede as societies globally recognized the preeminent importance of spiritual well-being. Each of his three final book projects— *Cosmology and Creation*, *The Greening of Faith*, and *Seeing Life Whole Again*—depended on some version of this view of history. For example, in *Cosmology and Creation*, he argued that a mechanistic modern science— which rests on seeing nature as a great machine—was being displaced by what he called "the new cosmology," a scientific practice that emphasized a basic, myth-like story about the origins of the universe. Similarly, in *The Greening of Faith*, he argued that the crisis of ecological catastrophe has overcome the old view of nature as a mere tool or instrument for our use and will force us to "see it again" as the totality in which we ourselves belong. In each of his texts, something about the present demanded that we pass beyond the modern obsession with scientific control and emerge on the other side of modernity with a renewed appreciation of the spiritual dimension.

My own dialogue with him shipwrecked most dramatically on the rocks of my father's post-modern messianism. I understood (though didn't always share) his negativity about the modern world and the inevitability that technological progress would necessarily lead to an ever-rising tide of spiritual impoverishment. But the simple trick where alternative new movements in science or politics would resolve the deadlock of modernity seemed, well, simplistic to me. I loved that my father became a great enthusiast in his later years for deep ecology and theoretical physics, each offering him, in one of his books, the promised way out of the iron cage of modernity. But I found the entire pageant of the post-modern tawdry. And I let him know it.

With the result that technology became a flag for the dysfunction of our personal dialogue, a marker of the limits past which conversation between philosopher father and philosopher son failed. My father could see that certain kinds of intellectual cheerleading bothered me, caused me to shut up and withdraw from the otherwise fruitful dialogue between us. I tried several times to explain my reservations about his messianic vision, using both scientific method and theological reasoning. But there was something about my father in those last years that made dialogue with him difficult. He was increasingly dogmatic, even if it was usually dogmatism for good causes with a good will.

As time went, the pregnant silence between my father and me that began with "the question concerning technology" (the title of Heidegger's most famous essay on the subject) radiated outward, cutting off most of the banter that earlier bound us so tightly together, even when we disagreed. I'm convinced we both suffered from this failure. I'm convinced we both measured our severely bounded later relationship against the intellectual solidarity and emotional closeness we enjoyed in my teen years.

In his very last years, technology also marked an ironic point of redemption between my father and me, a medium that let us revive our love unexpectedly. As often happens with elderly parents and their children, a clear moment arrived when my father and I switched roles from our previous natural order, when I became the caretaker and he the one cared for. For us, this exchange took place in that technological realm that had provoked our mutual alienation. I became his technical guru, the computer fix-it guy.

I think this exchange was powerful for both of us—though it commonly put us both in foul moods too. My father's dependence on technology for reading and hearing was complete. Beyond those expensive hearing aids, his Kindle and eventually his iPad extended his ability to read, with their capacity to blow up font sizes and increase brightness and contrast. Until the last year of his life, you could always find him with the tablet on his lap and text blown up to semaphoric dimensions. We kidded him about returning to children's books! Though capable of the nifty functions allowing him to read, these devices were mostly designed for the sighted—those able to distinguish the instructions and buttons that did not expand as generously as the texts he read. First the computer, then the Kindle, and finally the iPad became mere sites of frustration. Inevitably he hit "the wrong button" and found himself stuck in some incomprehensible digital cul-de-sac or, worse, the "blue screen of death."

When that happened, my father called *me*. Here, the role of fixit guy did its work on me. I bought into that role completely, rushing to his apartment at all hours to fix the iPad screen or the tv menu system. I also allowed this way of seeing myself to change my relationship to him. I noticed myself dreaming of technical fixes for him, which extended from the eye operation I convinced him to try at seventy-six, to broad research about resources for the aurally and visually impaired. Some solutions helped stave off that inevitable march toward the tiny room where he'd face death alone. Other solutions just immediately created geometrically multiplying technical problems. "How do I fix the God-damned sound-level on the blue-tooth headphones?" he screamed into the phone one day. But all of my repairs failed eventually, and that was, I think, what my father wanted.

At some deep, always unacknowledged level, the rebirth of our relationship as the old fogey and the computer repairman suited both of us. It allowed at least some daily transaction between us and a strange, transubstantiated tenderness that could survive even the old age and the steepening slope toward death that we both felt he was sliding along. Faced with failure—whether in a looming death or in the impossibility of pitching care as lovingly as I wished—technology proved a good substitute for gentle caring. Technology allowed us to act together again as we had not for many years.

I wonder if the gift of such common purpose isn't what my father tended to miss about the modern world in his view of technology as mere narcissistic control and obsession?

I don't blame him for missing things. After all, he was sadly isolated in that time. One thing in his life he was right about: the place we go to die, wherever that is, we go alone.

MEDITATION 11 BELIEF VERSUS FAITH

What is faith?

Family mythology relates two moments in my early childhood prophetic of my own future. Each involved a brush with one of the great philosophers of the 20th century. Later I'll tell you about my unfortunate incident in the lap of Hannah Arendt. For now, I'm concerned with the time in Chicago that the great Protestant theologian, Paul Tillich, tickled me in my baby carriage. I'm certainly happy that *one* of the great philosophers accepted me, even while a mere child, though by all acounts Tillich was an easy mark—an emotional man and affectionate father himself.

That Tillich blessed my childhood seems particularly appropriate, given my father's reliance on him. Of all the philosophical influences on my father, Tillich's was most important for the way my father actually lived. Such influence would surprise no scholar of my father's life. For several years as he wrote his dissertation, he trekked weekly from Evanston and Northwestern University to the South Side, where Tillich was a professor of theology at the University of Chicago. The influence I'm writing about here was really a transformation in life-attitude that manifested much later and guided my father increasingly long after Tillich's death.

A single powerful idea underlay the ethic Tillich imparted to my father: faith demands "the courage to be." In Tillich's famous book, *The Dynamics of Faith*, he writes that there must always be an element of *uncertainty* about faith as well as a particular sense of rightness. This uncertainty guarantees that living a faithful life involves a fundamental *courage*. *Just because* I don't really know the meaning of my life, I must gamble everything on my deepest belief about it. It takes courage to let go of the demand that we reduce everything to what we know, to a potential object of science, and accept the meaningfulness of whatever finitely presents itself to us without such a science. To repeatedly embrace uncertain life and develop *habits* of embracing the present is what Tillich called a "life of faith," and what my father tried to live.

Near the beginning of *Seeing Life Whole Again*, my father puts his philosophical vision in terms of such faith. Wonder, he writes, leads to a faith or particularly meaningful way of existing in…[our] universe and on just this particular planet we call "earth." Such faith is more a spiritual wisdom emerging from the very substance of our lives and expressed in stories than a set of beliefs or doctrines about God. Thus, attaining such faith takes more than the declaration of doctrines or even extensive theological arguments for such doctrines.

Faith is a form of life and not primarily a system of beliefs. From my father's perspective, a life of faith can form around any religious tradition or, more radically, no faith tradition at all. His "knight of faith" (Søren Kierkegaard's phrase) could be an *atheist* willing to deny any God's being but nonetheless committed to seeing life as wonder-filled. The important question for each of us is, "Have I lived a life of faith, a faithful life?" and not, "Have I convinced myself of God's existence or of any dogma specific to a particular religion?" An atheist could be perfectly faithful. For Dad himself, who confirmed that God does *not* exist as a being, this would be the only personal option for a life of faith.

A remarkable part of the manuscript of *Seeing Life Whole Again* is really an appendix, an e-mail dialogue between my father and his old friend, Frank, about what it means to live faithfully. Though my father doesn't explain this in his text, Frank was a key figure in the last third of his life—his Alcoholics Anonymous mentor. During the period when my father's deafness and blindness began to seriously hem in his life after his early forced retirement, he developed a drinking habit. Likely a key element in this was my mother's diagnosis of bipolar disorder, which demanded increasingly large amounts of his energy for holding *her* life in order. Whatever the causes, my father began to engage in occasional binge drinking that felt wildly and increasingly out of control. As often is the case with alcoholism, issues of control were uppermost in his experience. Was there some correspondence between my father's need to control the many apparently alien forces closing down his world and a drinking that felt like a hostile force breaching my father's walls?

Frank helped my father to interrupt this cycle of possession. Their dialogue quickly became something other than guidance through the dozen steps of AA's recovery program. I believe my father's extraordinary self-awareness about what *really* lay behind his ability to recover from alcoholism—he could see that the real issue was always letting go of his anxious need to control both his own and my mother's frailty and aging— led to an eventual *reversal* or balancing in his relationship to his mentor. My father had something to teach Frank about life too, and that's the story we read in the dialogue that appears in *Seeing Life Whole Again*.

This particularly valuable exchange reveals, better than the story about the Mormon missionaries, how my father actually dealt with the conflict between the way that he thought about *meaning* in life and the way most other people do. Maybe the best way into that conversation relates to the apparent equation of faith with "living meaningfully" at the beginning of the passage that I've quoted above. You might think that faith is just a synonym for "certainty." Like the person who discovers what the "meaning of life" is, the person of faith no longer finds doubt disturbing— so you would think. Such self-certainty stems from allaying any doubts about God or the specific dogmas of the believer's faith in God.

Frank begins from just such a set of assumptions. After noting initially to my father the importance of "letting go and trusting life" in order to live gracefully, he then writes:

> ...I most especially want a "God" who will somehow redeem this unfriendly world, one who will stand as a guarantee that this apparently hostile and chaotic world has a redeeming meaning and purpose. Since I first began, in college, to consider religious questions, I have always known this about myself—I want most especially to believe in this view that the world has meaning and purpose, what philosophers call a teleological view of the world. And the only way I can see to believe that view is through an even more basic religious belief of some sort. Only a God could give the world purpose. The world taken by itself would in my view be purposeless."

My father responds to Frank by pointing out how this demand sees the issues of meaning and faith from a peculiar, "objective" perspective, as though seeing the universe from outside in order to discern whether the intervention of a designer/creator has given it "meaning and purpose." For my father, such an attitude is fundamentally mistaken. As he writes,

> we seem to want to find a meaning to fit life taken to mean a reality external to each of us that we are contemplating in our imaginations. Here, spiritual meaning and purpose in life are treated like objective matters of fact that can be ascribed to life in general rather than to the unique particularity of your life or my life.

What we're looking for when we ask in that (objective) way if life is meaningful is actually not something that *could be* represented as a formula or objective truth. For my father, the search for "meaning" in this form is almost always a prelude to a *loss of faith*. If you're looking "out there" for meaning, you won't find it. Dad points this out to Frank and notes that the scientist always discovers truth through a method that distances itself from whatever it investigates, taking up a position "nowhere" to ensure objectivity. In this way, a scientific attitude can actively block the search for meaning, which must always be, in part, interior. The result of an objective starting point must be a fundamental skepticism. "Having developed ways of understanding the world that set aside meaning and value, we should not be surprised when ultimately they are incapable of finding them."

What then breaks the impasse in Frank's life and allows my father to return the favor Frank had done him with his drinking? It is an observation about the role of such control in my father's own earlier spiritual deadlock. The purpose of his seeking an "objective" meaning and the "certainty" or "security" it promises is what actually kept leading my father to "skepticism." The more he tried to secure a path to meaning, to God, to truth, and to establish it with unperturbable certainty, the more he actually doubted what he knew.

Against this path to skepticism, my father proposes the fundamental gesture of "giving up control." This happens by ceasing to imagine one can successfully complete the "desperate attempt to make life make sense through thought." The philosopher's efforts to answer the fundamental "why" and "how" questions about life can be either unhelpful (if they lead to "despairing lives emptied of just such meaning") or helpful (if "they bring us personally to the limits of reason and thereby open us to the direct experience of God by forcing us to encounter the mystery of that reality").

For my father, faith is not the certainty we gain through intellectual deduction or related empirical enquiry. Rather, faith is the sense of rightness that happens when we consciously and actively embrace what just happens to be in front of us—whether we're talking about the beauty of a day or a possibility for a career. Why call it faith if we can equate it to a purely intellectual certainty? My father loved to quote the great philosopher, mathematician, and religious thinker, Blaise Pascal, who warns us in his *Pensees* against that purely intellectual being, the "God of the Philosophers." Pascal insists instead that "the heart has its reasons that reason cannot know."

Faith is what comes from carefully and reflectively following one's heart.

When I hear about courage, my mind's eye immediately tends toward pictures of valor in battle or heroic struggles with natural calamity. Such a picture deceives us in reducing courage to its most physical and thus picturesque examples. Such a picture also seduces us into an overly active vision of the brave person. The call for images or pictures itself seduces us here too, inevitably favoring a courage that emerges in response to pre-defined challenges. The enemy emerges from the woods in full battle armor, the mountainside collapses in avalanche.

I learned of the more human courage of faith from my father, the courage to "put it on the line" once more every day, with every new twist and turn of one's own life, at moments when, at least to all appearances, nothing is happening. After my mother's death, he moved to be near me in Syracuse, New York. He lived in an apartment in The Nottingham, one of those retirement complexes that have sprung up around the country as his generation reaches old age. There he met and fell in love with Louise. This unexpected late-life romance made sense in part because of just how different Louise was from my mother. After my mother died, Dad spoke incessantly about his tiredness after more than fifty years of marriage. The information Dad began to let out about the last years made this mood perfectly understandable.

My mother was always difficult. Her brilliance had a certain brittleness that came out in obsessive anger, even vendettas against important persons in her life. I still remember my grandmother Sylvia cursing my mother on her deathbed. What began as apparently the ugliest relationship between a mother and a daughter in the history of humanity discolored all Barbara's other close relationships. But my father paid the price for her fragility as much as my mother did. He spent ever-increasing amounts of time and energy, particularly later, holding her life together, making sure that the rage that threatened to consume her did not. He succeeded in that. My mother died having made peace with all of us and, I think, herself. But the toll for that was my father's own spiritual and emotional exhaustion.

Which is just where Louise fits in. Louise described herself as a "simple soul," above all a mother from a conservative Christian family who took obvious pleasure in her children, grandchildren, and everyone else at The Nottingham. She enjoyed life without "doing" a lot. When my father and she took up, he looked at me and said, "I had no idea it could be so simple, Tom!"

Everybody loved Louise and loved my father and Louise together. They would sit holding hands on metal folding chairs on my father's little porch by one of the side-entrances to the building and chat with everybody coming and going by, perfectly happy to do little else. My father made it explicit to me, "I've decided to put it on the line one more time, Tom." And he had.

Ingredient to courage is the risk of failure—the rhino, or the enemy, might indeed kill you. My father's bravery was like that, exemplary of the courage of the elderly. Its risks were riskier than the cocksure moves of the young fighter pilot, the top gun, whose extraordinary, death-defying coordination only matches his obliviousness about just *what* he's taking those chances with. My father, on the other hand, knew what was at stake when he risked his life.

After just six months of closeness with Louise, his luck ran out. During several episodes, Louise had completely forgotten herself. She was found wandering along the road miles from The Nottingham or naked in the public hallways of their building. Those accelerating episodes led to a depressing diagnosis of incipient dementia and (rightly) convinced Louise's family to remove her to a nursing home for her own safety.

Arguably, my father chose to leave the world about four months before he actually ceased breathing, when Louise left their common home in the senior living community. Though he visited her in the nursing home nearby where she was relocated, the life they delicately began constructing together on the ashes of past marriages and families disintegrated, and my father fell into a deep funk. His own mental lapses—forgotten dates, dangling thoughts, and even wandering discourses—increased. He became obviously physically weaker, barely able to walk down to supper from his room without gasping for breath.

What seemed most different now was a depressive giving up—he could not gather his strength and try again. This mood was inseparable from what he himself called his "gradual decline" in those last months. That glide path to his own death wasn't any kind of cowardice. Indeed, for me, my father had long since earned whatever existential medal of honor one might imagine: too many were the times when he had proven himself —as first his hearing and then his sight failed, as my mother succumbed to the horrors of lung cancer, as he cheerfully departed the seacoast New Hampshire community in which he had anchored himself for fifty years for Syracuse—for me to doubt him then. Not cowardice but old age robbed my father of the means to come back from the loss of Louise; age robbed him of the strength, of the mere physical capacity, to accomplish once again the miracle of his remarkable faith.

MEDITATION 12 DEATH

Is to be human to die?

My father disdained the geeky scientific speculation about a future human immortality that has become popular in recent years. I remember how we chuckled on learning that baseball great Ted Williams spent some enormous sum on cryogenically freezing his head against the day when this hunk of dead brain-meat might be revived for eternal life. "Who would want the *head* of Ted Williams, anyhow?" my father asked. "Give me his hips and eyes!" My father treated the variations on this sci-fi theme with equal contempt: "uploading" human consciousness into some mega-computer and producing an effectively immortal "human consciousness" program.

Whatever consciousness is and to whatever extent we might ever simulate or even reproduce it in some deathless machined simulacrum of a human being, my father's point was simply that it would not be human if it were immortal. For him, being human is to die and to know that one will die.

Mystery, the experience that for him most humanizes us, depends upon how aware we are of our lives' basic *fragility.* In *Seeing Life Whole Again,* my father makes this point, connecting the moment of his own trauma with his later moment of transformative wonder. He references the later experience just after describing the BB gun accident. "Without the sense of the fragility and contingency of life to which the accident introduced me," he writes, "I felt I could not have broken through on that hillside overlooking the lake to the overwhelming experience of awe and wonder and thankfulness for life that occurred."

Only because his accident deeply impressed upon him the possibility that *he* might die, could he soon after see the world by Lake

Waushakum with the "glasses" of a very young mystic.

One explanation for my father's disdain for the Ted Williamses of the world lies in the importance he ascribed to that gentle vibration of a world announcing that it might altogether cease to be if given just a little too vigorous a shake. We can first open ourselves to wonder when our mood highlights experience as precious, at risk, potentially not there. The re-animated, immortal head-of-Ted (if I might) could be very smart indeed but it could never know wonder.

One reason that I find my father's passage about the BB gun accident so stirring is that he actually *never told* this story to me or my sister in person. He also minimized it in his published writing, only bringing it up briefly in *Cosmos and Creation*. His foolish adolescent behavior seems to have embarrassed him throughout his life—so much that he couldn't bring himself to share this "stupid" story. Here was a man who otherwise reveled in many other examples of his own laughableness. He loved to share tales of his foolish efforts in the German language or of his ineptitude at trying drugs, for example. But my sister and I never heard in person the full version of the BB gun story as it appears in the middle of *Seeing Life Whole*.

To explain his uncharacteristic reticence about the BB gun accident, let me include something else that he *does* say about it in the same passage I've quoted before. He says that the way his earlier experiences made the one by the lake possible was a kind of "re-writing."

> …My new sense of spiritual growth reached back into my past to re-construe that earlier accident. Now, it was not just the most dreadful event in my life—although my earlier memory of it as such was still clearly intact. Now, I remembered it as a necessary condition for experiencing what I came to call "God" on that hillside two years later. Thus, I then came to see it as a gift without which my life could not have been graced in the way that it was.

I suspect that, as is typical of experiences demanding such therapeutic re-writing, the BB gun accident was a genuine *trauma* in my father's life—an experience that so overwhelmed him that he could only face it, remember it, in an act that transformed it, "re-wrote" it. He transformed a horrible, life-threatening situation into something other than the pure pain that it originally was. Such working through a trauma allows it to take its place, still with difficulty, in the register of normal, remembered events. It even allowed him to include the trauma in the pre-history of the story he cared most about, the story of his experience of God.

Often we speak of a sense of "nausea" when trying to recall something like that, and generally we do our best not to let our minds dwell on the experience. Afflictions like PTSD often emerge when the mind cannot *stop* remembering a moment of trauma—the bomb exploding, the stick coming down on one's head, the barrel of the BB gun firing into one's eye. PTSD (or as they called it in Freud's day, "shell shock,") dooms the victim to awaken every night screaming as the broken record of that moment plays itself over and over. Even my tale-loving father preferred not talking about the details of his accident in an otherwise storied life!

The philosopher who most influenced my father's insight here was, once again, Martin Heidegger, the highly problematic but vital and brilliant thinker from the Black Forest in Germany whose greatest work, *Being and Time,* has at its very center an ethics for how to live with precisely the kind of trauma so vital to my father's path into philosophy. Heidegger insists that *anxiety*, unbeknownst to us, actually carries our everyday awareness of our own impending and inevitable death.

What does anxiety have to do with the experience of trauma?

Heidegger writes that in anxiety, I, first of all, have an experience that, in everyday language, normally lacks a definite object. As evidence of this, contrast how we use "anxiety" as opposed to "fear." In English as in Heidegger's native German, "fear" can be a transitive verb. Thus, "I fear the wolf." On the other hand, to express anxiety, we always use the phrase "I have anxiety" or "I feel anxiety" or "I feel anxious." Anxiety's "object" seems undefined, indefinite, and so also is our response to it in comparison to our response to fear. We flee that wolf. We do not know how exactly to get away from the looming object that makes us anxious. Precisely because it won't come into focus as a definite object, I am often paralyzed in anxiety.

In *Being and Time,* Heidegger argues that the reason for this uncanniness of anxiety's object is that, really, it represents ourselves, like the shadow of one's own body perceptible through the corner of the eye. Anxiety subsists in an indefinite sense (perhaps better, a mood) of threat that existence might eventually cease to be. Heidegger writes of coming "face to face with the 'nothing' of the possible impossibility of (our) own existence."

Heidegger's insight when speaking about such anxiety is that, of all the ways that we can think about death, even about our *own* deaths, this anxious nausea is the most important, the true key to our humanity. We tend to think of our consciousness of our own deaths as an extension of our knowledge that others die. We usually imagine the inert and lifeless body, the coffin, and then put ourselves in it. We see death in others and project the same in ourselves. But Heidegger's point is that anxiety is actually the vital phenomenon of our consciousness, each of us, that we will die. Each of us has some experience or set of experiences whose presence in life is similar to the BB gun accident for my father—something or somethings that haunt us, make us anxious, sometimes even drive us to break down.

Heidegger's key idea was that this experience brings with it a particular value, an ethics, about what we should do *in response* to our anxiety before death. Such anxiety demands that we take our lives in hand, take responsibility for an otherwise disastrous crisis in our consciousness. "Get a grip, man!" we say to the anxious person before us, frozen in impotent paralysis. We all know that defeating our "deer in the headlights" moments demands more than will. It demands some transformation of the experience that so threatens us, some placement of it inside a larger, meaning-generating project—a life helping others, or painting the beauty of the world, or teaching philosophy.

My father lived precisely that insight, that the presence of death as trauma in each of our lives demands we bravely "re-write" the traumatic moment and weave it into a forward-looking life project. His accident constituted a test for him, both a danger and an opportunity. Anxiety demanded the labor of re-construing this past into a wondrous, new present. The paralysis of his anxious near-death experience required that he grow into the kind of person who could celebrate the ephemeral wonder of existing.

Quietly, without the fanfare that he so joyfully blew when it came to his many less significant moments of foolishness or weakness, he spent the rest of his life *doing philosophy*. That was the ongoing form of *his* therapy for anxiety and death. In gently polishing the surfaces of wonder and mystery in his own life and using the resultant gem to cast light on a thousand dialogues, to build, also, a full and meaningful life, my father staved off the mighty blast foreshadowed by the discharge of his toy weapon at eleven. He fought it off all through my mother's death and through the gradual but inexorable defeat of his senses. Philosophy gained him a strange, lifelong cheerfulness, a shit-eating grin that survived even the many devastations of his old age.

Five weeks before he died, my father fell. He minimized the event, saying that he slipped a little on a towel. But as I discussed what happened with him and with the woman who helped him to take care of his life at The Nottingham, it became clear that he had spent several hours on the floor, that she had found him then lying there covered in his own waste. Sharon lifted and cleaned him. In general, she protected him from his own indignities and she conspired with him, too, to play down that event so that my wife Rachel, my daughter Sophie, and I could go off to Boston for some surgery that my wide needed. We tried to convince him to come along. He would have none of that, saying that he didn't feel that strong and wanted time to rest.

The call came sooner than even I expected, right after the successful completion of Rachel's procedure. My father had fallen again. This time he was so completely incoherent when found the next day that they had rushed him off to the hospital in an ambulance. I hastened back to Syracuse, leaving Rachel recovering with Sophie and the rest of Rachel's family, only to find my father barely conscious. The doctors said that he suffered at least one serious stroke. He could not speak or, really, think very clearly.   Over the next days, his condition improved a little; after a week or so he could utter full sentences and the slurring of his speech receded. However, his mental confusion just came to the forefront. Not only was my father confused about pretty much everything, he could not really keep even simple thoughts in his head. He took to wandering from room to room in the hospital, hastening his discharge to the nursing home where he soon died.

I was deeply shocked when I first saw him on my return from Boston. More than his death, what upset me was the confusion in his eyes when I showed up. I don't think he recognized me at first. His doctors were convinced his loss of mental function was permanent. Some three weeks later, his death itself came as a relief. My appearance by his bedside clearly upset him, drawing his attention to his own lostness, his own confusion. He grunted and cried. Only when he took my hand did a look of relief come into his face. This was a new experience of my father—the child needing reassurance. Or, rather, the person facing death alone and needing orientation in his own life, the life that was finishing.

I've written of the long truce between my father and me that kept philosophy mostly in the background. Something about the situation in the hospital room in those last few weeks annulled that agreement: he needed to touch the life that he had led, a life in philosophy, and only I could help him to do that. As my father's coming death threatened to overwhelm us both, a job for me began to take shape. Was it his gift to me or my own gift to myself?

It turned out that a relatively new film about one of Dad's existentialist heroes was recently available on video, Margarethe von Trotta's *Hannah Arendt*. So I set the film up on my father's oversized iPad. Lying with him on the narrow cot, I watched it with him from beginning to end. He went in and out of consciousness, but each time he awoke he looked intently at the screen and squeezed my hand.

A bit of background: Arendt, a Jewish philosopher and one-time lover of (yes, once again) Martin Heidegger, had herself fled the Nazis for New York where she began to teach for that famous home of continental philosophers-in-exile, the New School for Social Research. The Israelis' 1960 capture of Adolph Eichmann, perhaps *the* primary administrator of the "final solution," and his subsequent prosecution led Arendt to write a series of "reports" from Jerusalem about the trial. First serialized in the *The New Yorker* magazine and then published as a book, Arendt's *Eichmann in Jerusalem: The Banality of Evil*, depended directly on Heidegger's ethics, demanding that one should authentically acknowledge one's own death, re-construing it so as to transform it into a gift.

Eichmann presented himself in the trial as the merest bureaucrat, the guy who, "just following orders," made the trains run on time (to Auschwitz, as it turned out). For Arendt, he represented what comes from ignoring that imperative and failing to attend to the presence of death that allows one to live meaningfully. Lacking anything genuinely numinous in his life, Eichmann became a cipher who served the machine of death that was Nazism—an efficient, "good," and strangely "happy" servant of the master, proud of the quality of his work on the "final solution."

Such was Arendt's account of Eichmann. Von Trotta's movie—which comes about as close to filming philosophy as one can get—tells the story of the period from 1960 through 1964, when Arendt published this story and reaped the whirlwind of world disapproval. Many mistook her work as minimizing the true evil of the Nazis and of Eichmann in particular. For *her* Eichmann (and, honestly, the figure who presented himself at the famous trial) was no sadist, no devil, no cruel mass-murderer reveling in feasts of human blood. He was only somebody who *failed* to re-write the traumatic shadow in the corner of his eye. The world, particularly the world of those in New York whose families included riders (and many survivors of riders) on those efficiently dispatched death trains, could not entertain such a grey and lifeless picture of evil as "banal." Thus, *Hannah Arendt* narrates the storm of anger that Arendt faced after the publication of *Eichmann in Jerusalem*.

My father and, in a sense, I both knew the Arendt of this period, or just after. Soon after his arrival at the University of New Hampshire in 1964, my father invited Arendt to speak there. She came and of course we hosted a cocktail party for her. Family mythology has it that five-year-old me, a lap child if ever there was one, decided to snuggle up with the guest of honor. Arendt, who hated children, had squirmed and immediately pushed me off her lap.

The film brought Arendt, the living person, the prickly, unpleasant but also brilliant acquaintance of my father who had graced our home that evening, back to both of us. All of this is just to say that *Hannah Arendt*, meticulously researched and produced in perfect 60s style, brought my father momentarily back to himself, and back to *us* and our long life together. He couldn't speak, but, as I lay beside him on his hospital bed watching the film, I sensed his relief. Though in bed, he had his feet on the ground again, at least for the moment. He squeezed my hand again and watched, tears in his eyes. He was there and, above all, there *with me,* for the first time in years. For all the terror of death, it was a terror that he had prepared for throughout the entirety of his good life. His possibilities were clear. My father was home again.

Afterword: The Death of Paul

Heidegger, Paul Brockelman's intellectual "father," famously introduced an Aristotle seminar with the terse words, "Aristotle was born, philosophized for a while, and died"—substituting this formulation for the customary biography that even professors in Germany feel obligated to give before diving into purely philosophical questions. As the book you've just been reading testifies, I disagree with Heidegger here. When it comes to my father, only his life can make sense of an intellectual path that, taken on its own, many might find unremarkable—typical of a generation, but not really groundbreaking or surprising. To *know* my father was to philosophize with him. I doubt many would really get to the remarkableness of the philosophy, though, without finding it through him.

Still, on the whole, I'd have to agree with Heidegger when it comes to death itself. Better to say little or nothing than to drone on about the unremarkable. With death, we really want to see what we know *cannot be seen*. We want a death-scene worthy of the life that this man lived. And the death that each of us really knows isn't about that. Mostly, the best that I can do is to show a gap: two months to the day before, my father and I had argued about the "objectivity" of his view of Christianity. He was in a foul mood, but as sharp as a tack in his recollection of the so-called *Gnostic Gospels* that had transformed the historian's view of early Christianity. On a Tuesday, three weeks after his release from the hospital where they took him after that second stroke, he restlessly wandered the halls of the recovery nursing home, occasionally stumbling into the rooms of other patients without being aware that he was doing so.

It's important to insist that, even in his brief senility, my father was always a sweet man. The nurses saw this. He would shuffle around the halls with a smile on his face and he seemed genuinely affectionate if even sometimes inappropriately so. He was not in control of much of anything in his life. They had to tie him to his bed to prevent him from violating the privacy of others. As he looked blankly into my eyes across the table over an institutional turkey dinner, he ignored his food and repeated endlessly the only sentence he'd successfully gotten out (badly slurred) after the stroke: "Things look really bad, Tom, really bad!"

Such a chasm opened up—as deep and un-crossable as change is sudden—between the man whose career sprung from his mind and his spirit and the one who muttered at me across the table that day. My sister Mira rushed east from Oregon, still naïvely hoping to plan for a visit from him as he had promised just weeks before. Together we shook our heads at his lack of daily progress, at the increasing certainty that he faced the life of senile indignity that we so hoped he would avoid. It looked like a future of bed pans and nursing homes, my father the merest whisper of himself. I only comforted myself by knowing that he had never really been just a "head" guy and that the sweetness (now drained of complexity and wit, admittedly) that always characterized him still did—a minimally just outcome for a man who so consciously dedicated his life to remaining open to experience and people. Still, it was hard to witness that absence of him, that stupendous decline from the man he had so recently been. Maybe the best image of my father's death would be this lack of the image of him as we all knew him. One day he was just gone.

Nonetheless, there was a final scene, one that helps to explain the book you are just finishing. That very day, after the abysmal turkey dinner, Mira had just departed for the airport and her flight home when my father suddenly began to convulse. The on-duty nurse explained to me the likely cause, pulmonary embolism, while the various emergency forces rushed to his bedside, one of the many possible horrific "gifts" related to his heavy regime of mutually negating medications, and an often-fatal event. I called Mira back from the road.

Within twenty minutes he was dead.

Mira and I lay with my father as he struggled for life in those last minutes, holding his hand, comforting him. But I remember an image of him so vividly, his chest heaving as he threw off his clothes and covers. There was something extraordinarily baroque about him—something that demanded Caravaggio or even Rubens to capture. Flushed and ruddy-cheeked, his face somehow had the definition of those El Greco paintings that my father loved. So odd, noticing that his death took on this baroque aesthetic quality even as we endured the agony of losing him. It was as though, in dying, Dad renewed his great struggle, came up with the energy that had otherwise failed him. As he died, we saw for a moment something terrifyingly authentic in our father, something so nakedly alive and brave that it could not last.

And, like so much baroque painting, dramatic—almost melodramatic.

My father's life was storied, demanded telling, an imperative to which he, a natural storyteller, always responded. Of course, panicked and broken by his sudden collapse and death (a suddenness that we only later celebrated, thinking of the suffering it saved him), no thought of it crossed my mind. But later, weeks after the memorial service, as I held the manuscript of *Seeing Life Whole Again* in my lap, the idea for the book you have before you formed, itself fluttering moth-like around the weak picture of my father's final, baroque struggles.

Actually, I later realized that the thrashing body we held on the day of my father's death brought me back to one final story about him. Since I grew up near Boston, the family cultural expedition would often take us to the Isabella Stuart Gardner Museum, redoubt of Boston Brahminism and the scene of several formative events in my youth. One such event occurred when, only ten or so, as best I can tell, on entering the famous Dutch Room, my younger sister Mira (who was quite young, six or seven) and I ran up to an impressive painting of a man in gleaming armor and exclaimed, "Daddy, it's you!" An oil portrait of a nobleman by a young Rubens, the painting did resemble my father, though revealing something different about him than the melancholy photographs of Lincoln adorning our bulletin boards at home. If this were Paul Brockelman, then it was a heroic and, yes, baroque version of him—an active and courageous hero but also a human being amongst men!

In my mind, my father on his deathbed was "sitting" for his portrait as the Earl of Arundel, hero of many lives. It would be a portrait that I alone, philosopher son and heir to the house of philosophy he bequeathed, could sketch. And it would be a picture that my father deserved, a true likeness both to honor him and forward the causes he fought for. Forward Paul Brockelman, brave soldier of philosophy!

Peter Paul Rubens, *Portrait of the Earl of Arundel* (1629-30). Gardner Museum, Boston

References and Further Inquiry:

1. Books:

Arendt, Hannah. *Eichmann in Jerusalem: A Report on the Banality of Evil*. Penguin Classics. New York, N.Y: Penguin Books, 2006.

———. *The Origins of Totalitarianism*. New York: Harcourt, Brace and Co, 1951.

Aristotle, J. A. K. Thomson, Hugh Tredennick, and Aristotle. *The Nicomachean Ethics*. Further rev. ed. Penguin Classics. London, Eng. ; New York, N.Y: Penguin Books, 2004.

Bakewell, Sarah. *At the Existentialist Café: Freedom, Being, and Apricot Cocktails with Jean-Paul Sartre, Simone de Beauvoir, Albert Camus, Martin Heidegger, Karl Jaspers, Edmund Husserl, Maurice Merleau-Ponty and Others*. New York: Other Press, 2016.

Brockelman, Paul T. *Cosmology and Creation: The Spiritual Significance of Contemporary Cosmology*. New York: Oxford University Press, 1999.

———. *Existential Phenomenology and the World of Ordinary Experience: An Introduction*. Lanham, MD: University Press of America, 1980.

———. *The Inside Story: A Narrative Approach to Religious Understanding and Truth*. Albany: State University of New York Press, 1992.

Carroll, John E., Paul T. Brockelman, Mary Westfall, and Bill McKibben, eds. *The Greening of Faith: God, the Environment, and the Good Life*. Twentieth-Anniversary edition. Durham, New Hampshire: University of New Hampshire Press, 2016.

Hadot, Pierre, and Arnold I. Davidson. *Philosophy as a Way of Life: Spiritual Exercises from Socrates to Foucault*. Malden, MA: Blackwell, 1995.

Handelman, Susan A. *The Slayers of Moses: The Emergence of Rabbinic Interpretation in Modern Literary Theory*. SUNY Series on Modern Jewish Literature and Culture. Albany: State University of New York Press, 1982.

Heidegger, Martin. *Being and Time*. Oxford: Blackwell, 1967.

———. *The Question Concerning Technology, and Other Essays*. New York: Garland Pub, 1977.

James, William. *The Varieties of Religious Experience*. 1st Vintage Books/The Library of America ed. New York: Vintage Books/Library of America, 1990.

Kaag, John J. *American Philosophy: A Love Story*. First [edition]. New York: Farrar, Straus and Giroux, 2016.

———. *Hiking with Nietzsche: On Becoming Who You Are*. First [edition]. New York: Farrar, Straus, and Giroux, 2018.

Kierkegaard, Søren. *Fear and Trembling*. Penguin Classics. Harmondsworth, Middlesex, England : New York, N.Y., U.S.A: Penguin Books ; Viking Penguin, 1985.

Alastair Hannay, and Søren Kierkegaard. *Concluding Unscientific Postscript to the Philosophical Crumbs*. Cambridge Texts in the History of Philosophy. Cambridge, UK ; New York: Cambridge University Press, 2009.

Marx, Karl, Robert C. Tucker, and Friedrich Engels. *The Marx-Engels Reader*. New York: Norton, 1972.

Maugham, W. Somerset. *Sheppey: A Play in Three Acts*. London: W. Heinemann, ltd, 1933.

Nietzsche, Friedrich Wilhelm, and Walter Arnold Kaufmann. *Thus Spoke Zarathustra: A Book for All and None*. Compass Books C196. New York: Viking Press, 1966.

Nussbaum, Martha C. *Cultivating Humanity: A Classical Defense of Reform in Liberal Education*. Cambridge, Mass: Harvard University Press, 1997.

Plato, Edith Hamilton, and Huntington Cairns. *The Collected Dialogues of Plato, Including the Letters*. Bollingen Series 71. New York: Pantheon Books, 1961.

Sartre, Jean-Paul. *Being and Nothingness*. New York : Avenel, N.J: Gramercy Books ; distributed by Random House, 1994.

Sartre, Jean-Paul, and Robert Baldick. *Nausea*. Harmondsworth, Middlesex, England: Penguin, 1965.

Tillich, Paul. *Dynamics of Faith*. 1st Perennial classics ed. Perennial Classics. New York: Perennial, 2001.

———. *The Courage to Be*. 3rd edition. New Haven: Yale University Press, 2014.

2. Films

Herzog, Werner. *The Enigma of Kaspar Hauser*, 1974
von Trotta, Margarethe. *Hannah Arendt*, 2012

3. Images

Portrait of Paul Brockelman painted by Adeline Goldminc-Tronzo (with permission of the artist)

Title page of the manuscript, *Seeing Life Whole Again*, by Paul Brockelman

Paul and Barbara: Wedding Photo 1958

Paul Brockelman addresses the students of the University of New Hampshire: May 5, 1970.

Abe and Abe-y Baby: The Lincoln Resemblance!

Barbara and Paul in Yugoslavia: 1972

Peter Paul Rubens, Portrait of the Earl of Arundel (1629-30): Gardner Museum, Boston